Minnesota's State Capitol

Minnesota Historical Society Press

Minnesota's State Capitol

The Art and Politics of a Public Building

Neil B. Thompson

Foreword by *Elmer L. Andersen*

www.mnhs.org/mhspress

The Minnesota Historical Society Press is a member of the Association of American University Presses.

Manufactured in Canada

10 9 8 7 6 5 4 3

♾ The paper used in this publication meets the minimum requirements of the American National Standard for Information Sciences—Permanence for Printed Library Materials, ANSI Z39.48-1984.

Frontispiece: Senators meeting in their new chamber in April 1905 beneath Edwin H. Blashfield's mural of explorers at the source of the Mississippi River

International Standard Book Number 0-87351-085-2

Library of Congress Cataloging-in-Publication Data

Thompson, Neil B.
Minnesota's State Capitol: the art and politics of a public building.

1. St. Paul. State Capitol. 2. Gilbert, Cass, 1859-1934. 3. Politics in art.

na4413.s24t45   917.76´581   74–4326

Minnesota's State Capitol was designed and set in Adobe Caslon type by Dennis Anderson, Duluth, Minnesota, and printed by Friesens, Altona, Manitoba.

Contents

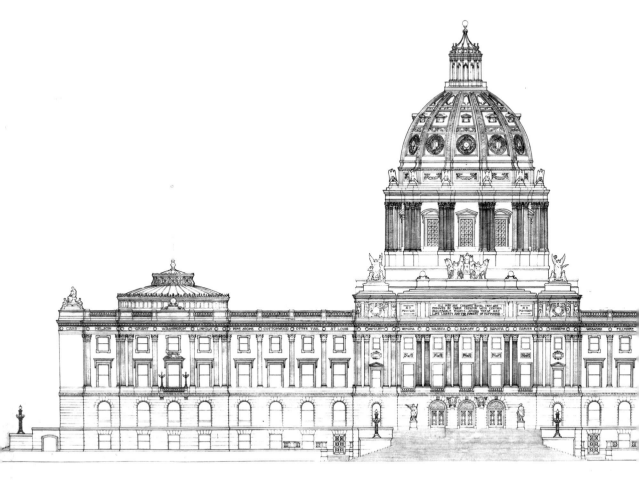

Gilbert's ink rendering of proposed capitol design, about 1895

Foreword

SEEN AT NIGHT, LIGHTED, Minnesota's state capitol is a glowing jewel on a carpet of dark velvet. It is so noble in concept and distinguished in accomplishment that one can be pardoned for thinking there could not have been any argument about any detail of its design and construction. Yet, argument there was—on the commission entrusted to provide a new capitol for the state, as well as among legislators and citizens. Neil Thompson has done a careful job of tracing the project from its inception to its completion, a story he reconstructs from the records of the commission and the newspapers of the day.

The original legislative appropriation for the capitol was two million dollars. But it was quickly apparent that this would be an insufficient amount to produce the caliber of building people wanted. So, without much opposition, the legislature voted another million. Delay in awarding some contracts brought the project into the economic boom of the early 1900s. Prices and wages increased substantially, and once again the commission felt that if the interior were to be completed in keeping with the opulence of the exterior, more money was needed. One and a half million was suggested, causing some hesitation and debate, but the sum was granted with little recorded opposition.

The most vituperative opposition to the capitol project came with the announcement of the stone to be used in the superstructure. From the beginning different quarries in Minnesota competed to supply stone for the project. The most careful study indicated that Georgia marble was best suited for the desired effect and was also the lowest priced option. But when it was announced as a choice for the superstructure, a tempest of protest ensued. (Quarry representatives used such expressions as "driving a dagger into the heart of the industry.") Ultimately, Minnesota stone was used in the foundation, exterior stairways, and the interior, but through the perseverance of architect Cass Gilbert and commission vice chairman Channing Seabury, the choice of Georgia marble prevailed.

Cass Gilbert was chosen after two rounds of design elimination and a final decision to invite proposals from selected architects. The choice was masterful. The Minnesota capitol started a career path that was to take Gilbert to national and international distinction as the designer of such buildings as New York's Woolworth Building and the Supreme Court Building in Washington, D.C. He not only had brilliance of technical competence but also a rare ability to harmonize differences and win his way on important decisions. Channing Seabury devoted 14 years of his life to the project, unselfishly, devotedly, and strongly supporting the architect and guarding the expenditure of public funds.

The first event marking the capitol's completion celebrated the placement in the rotunda of regimental flags belonging to the Minnesota units that participated in famous battles during the War Between the States and the Spanish American War. It was clear the flags represented Minnesota's pride in and

Postcard view looking up Cedar Street toward the new white capitol and (to its left) the tower of old (second) capitol, 1904

devotion to those who had served in these conflicts and the recognition of the suitability of the grand new capitol to preserve and display the banners.

The finished building not only provided dignified and beautiful spaces for the state's constitutional officers, legislature, and judiciary, but more especially it projected the people's dream of a capitol worthy of the great state that was to be. It is remarkable that one hundred years later, Minnesotans are filled with the same pride in the design and execution of a grand scheme as they were when the capitol was built.

Neil Thompson's splendid account was first published in 1974 and here is reissued for the 100th anniversary of the capitol. It is a valuable recounting of the tireless work that went into the final creation that is still worthy of the pride of a modern state.

ELMER L. ANDERSEN

Elmer L. Andersen served in the capitol's Senate Chamber from 1949 to 1957 and the Governor's Office from 1961 to 1963.

A crowd gathered on June 14, 1905, for the ceremonial transfer of flags to the new capitol. The prominent gilded quadriga has not yet been installed.

Prologue

LATE INTO the night of January 2, 1905, thousands of people crowded through the halls of the new Minnesota State Capitol. In language typical of turn-of-the-century journalism, the *Minneapolis Tribune* reported on January 3 that they "drank in the beauties of the decorations, and grew enthusiastic over the wonderful mural art which adorns the halls and legislative chambers." The "incandescent" light, marble columns, Kasota stone interior, crystal chandelier in the rotunda, wrought-iron gophers and showy ladyslippers on the stairways and columns drew excited comment. The seminudity of some of the classical female figures in the murals probably drew a different kind of comment. For Minnesotans, still living on the edge of the frontier, that new year was a time of pride and excitement and the beginning of a feeling of permanence. Some in the crowd could remember the first meeting of the state legislature in 1858 in the old territorial capitol at Exchange and Wabasha streets in St. Paul; now they were viewing a fine monument that expressed their concept of the sovereign state and their ideal of public magnificence with its blend of ancient architectural form and modern engineering skill. It was, indeed, a moment to remember.

Public buildings in the United States have shown a remarkable conformity to the ideal fixed in the imagination by the federal Capitol in Washington, D.C. Until Bertram Grosvenor Goodhue began building the "Tower of the Plains" for Nebraska in 1922, most state capitols had imitated Thomas Jefferson's ideal of a restrained version of the architectural monuments of ancient Rome.[1] The arguments for casting public taste in such a mold were simple. Rome represented the ancient glory of republican government; its grandeur resulted from the power of the nation; its public buildings were a reflection of the nation and its place in history. The United States of America would, by following Roman principles, present man with a modern display of republicanism and its glories. In the public mind propriety demanded that public buildings should reflect the power and sovereignty of the nation. To the celebrants in St. Paul, as the new year began, the new capitol was a fitting monument to those canons.

The mood of the people of Minnesota at the beginning of the twentieth century was one of growing prosperity and fervent nationalism. The United States had survived the moral and constitutional crises of the Civil War. The names of Chickamauga, Nashville, Chattanooga, Vicksburg, and Gettysburg were linked in their minds with the valor of Minnesota regiments. The United States had placed itself among the powers of the world by acquiring an overseas empire in the Philippines in the Spanish-American War. The depression of 1893 had become a thing of memory. Farmers had a good year in 1904. Corn was selling for $.46 and wheat for $1.15 a bushel; hog and cattle prices were $4.00 a hundred and up. The commodity markets were rather bullish now that reports of too much rain on the pampas of the Argentine allayed fears of a bumper crop of wheat in that quarter of the world.[2]

Politics had become quieter since Ignatius Donnelly's Farmers' Alliance party had waned in the wake of his defeat for a state Senate seat in 1894. Yes, they gossiped on the street corners, the Democrats had just elected John A. Johnson, that newspaper editor from St. Peter, as governor to succeed Republican Samuel R. Van Sant, but after all, Johnson was the first governor who had been born in Minnesota. Besides he was only the third Democrat in the history of the state to reach the governorship—third, that is, if you wanted to count the legendary Henry H. Sibley who had been the first governor. Anyway, the Republican farmers in the southern third of Minnesota had maintained their control of the Senate.

Everything considered, 1905 was a good year for Minnesotans. They had confidence in their government and they were prosperous. Their new capitol was just the thing to express their place in the sun. The *Minneapolis Tribune* summed up the matter on January 8 when it proclaimed that the statehouse "is not an art gallery; it is not a building constructed for show or to satisfy the artistic sense of the designers or builders. It is an everlasting monument to the sovereignty of the state."

The physical location, the architectural style, and the interior design all contributed to the symbolic significance of the grand new structure located on low, rounded Wabasha Hill (it was already being referred to as "Capitol Hill") near downtown St. Paul. To the southwest on St. Anthony Hill, Archbishop John Ireland was planning a new Catholic cathedral.[3] Thus monuments to both church and state would soon dominate the skyline of St. Paul, a city that had grown like Topsy around the settlement Pierre Parrant had fortuitously established on the flood plain of the Mississippi River in 1840. Perhaps the only deliberate element in the symbolism of the site was its location on University Avenue, the principal street linking the state's two major population centers, the Twin Cities of St. Paul and Minneapolis.[4] A third element unconsciously completed the visual symbolism of church, state, and business, when in 1931 the First National Bank of St. Paul erected a thirty-two-story skyscraper that dominated the city's skyline for the next several decades.

If the site was symbolically fortuitous, the architectural design of the building conformed to the American tradition. The Board of State Capitol Commissioners reported in 1901 that a "canvass of public sentiment showed that a central dome and rotunda must be part of the design, and that the people would not be satisfied with any other." The design selected by the commission had followed the public's sentiment; the central dome was flanked by wings that gave symmetry to the front of the structure. The classical triangular pediment was entirely eliminated, and the whole structure was dominated by a somewhat smaller and more graceful version of the dome on St. Peter's Basilica in Rome designed by Michelangelo. With a modicum of statuary and a grand quadriga featuring three heroic figures and four horses above the main entrance, the building presented a strong and balanced effect whose detail was revealed gradually as one approached it. Both the *St. Paul Pioneer Press* and the *Minneapolis Tribune* gave it editorial approval early on. The lack of controversy over the design suggests a period of stable social values in which it was possible to select an agreeable plan with a minimum of dissension.[5]

The exterior, happily, reflected the form of the interior to become a symbol in stone for the republican form of government practiced in the United States. The main entry opened directly into the public rotunda, which then flowered into all other parts (and functions) of the building. Grand staircases to the left and to the right provided access to the second floor, and around them the main corridors of the first floor invited easy passage. Through those corridors the citizen could reach all the principal officers of the executive branch. To the west off the left corridor lay the governor's suite with its ornate reception room and offices. To the north lay the rooms of the attorney general. The opposite corridor gave access to the state treasurer and the secretary of state. Thus the constitutional officers were grouped in a manner the capitol's architect believed would "best accommodate the business of the State officers."[6]

The staircase from the rotunda led, on the left side, directly into the Senate Chamber, placing the weight of that body directly over the head of the governor. The right staircase rose up to the Supreme Courtroom, separating that part from the other branches of the government while at the same time including it as a part of the whole. Entry to the House of Representatives was gained through a corridor that connected to the rotunda and to the main entrance of the building and, in turn, to the view of the city of St. Paul. Thus the House, as the largest governmental body, faced the people directly though symbolically. The design was remarkably open both to sight and to access. Each branch and each office had its bailiwick, but the constitutional officers were placed in a businesslike position on the lower floor, while the legislative and judicial branches occupied a more aloof position emphasizing their deliberative functions. The physical design of the building suggested a relationship within the government that was more truly reflective of popular thought than any constitutional description. On the whole, the new building radiated a sense of Victorian propriety satisfying to the state's citizens. The feeling for color, ornament, and richness was stately and restrained, while the American notion of functionalism was apparent in the arrangement of space.

If the totality presented something of the usual, however, the symmetry of the design, the integration of the ornamentation, the sense of unity in the entire structure, and the relative shortness of the period of construction (fourteen years from approval to completion) were unusual for public buildings in the United States up to that time.[7] The ornament on Capitol Hill was a tribute to its architect, Cass Gilbert, and to the patience, skill and taste of the man who served as vice-president of the Board of State Capitol Commissioners, Channing Seabury. For Gilbert the project was the steppingstone to an important place in the contemporary architectural world. For Seabury it was a public service. From these two men the people of Minnesota received a legacy that they have long cherished and which they can maintain, in the perspective of man's short time sense, forever.

Minnesota's State Capitol

Members of the Board of State Capitol Commissioners who served from 1895 to 1905.
From left to right: Edgar Weaver, John De Laittre, Charles H. Graves, Channing Seabury,
George A. Du Toit, Eben E. Corliss, and Henry W. Lamberton.

1 · The Site and the Design

As THE NATION WAS SLIDING into the third longest depression in its history, the people of Minnesota undertook a building project of the first magnitude, a capitol that would mark their emergence from the frontier into the modern world of urbanization. The initiative came from the 1891 legislature, where Senator Frank G. McMillan, Democrat from Hennepin County, offered a resolution calling for the appointment of a committee to investigate the need for a new building. The duly appointed committee filed its report on February 3, 1893, recommending construction. Bills were subsequently introduced by Senator William B. Dean and Representative Hiler H. Horton, both of St. Paul, and approved by the 1893 legislature committing Minnesota to expend not less than $2,000,000 for a new statehouse to be erected in St. Paul under the direction of a Board of State Capitol Commissioners to be named by the governor. Governor Knute Nelson wasted no time. He consulted the authors of the bills that had gained legislative approval and made his appointments to the board. He selected as commissioners one man from each of the state's seven congressional districts.[1]

Eleven men would serve on the board during the fourteen years of its existence. The seven initially chosen by Nelson were: Henry W. Lamberton of Winona (First District), James McHench of Martin County (Second District), George A. Du Toit of Chaska (Third District), Channing Seabury of St. Paul (Fourth District), John De Laittre of Minneapolis (Fifth District), Charles H. Graves of Duluth (Sixth District), and Eben E. Corliss of Fergus Falls (Seventh District). McHench died early in 1895 before the real work of the project began. He was succeeded by Daniel Shell of Worthington, who in turn was replaced after a few months by Edgar Weaver of Mankato. Weaver represented the Second District on the board for the remaining twelve years. Turnover also occurred in the First District representatives. Henry W. Lamberton served until his death in 1905, when his position was filled by John Ludwig, a Winona hotel owner. After Ludwig died in 1906, Henry M. Lamberton, an attorney and son of the original appointee, represented the district.[2]

All three men from the First District were Democrats, as was Du Toit of the Third. The other seven appointees were Republicans. The average age of the eleven men who served during the board's existence was 55. The youngest of the eleven (Weaver) was forty-three at the time of his appointment; the eldest (McHench) was sixty-nine.

A clear reminder of the nearness of the pioneer era to the Minnesota of the 1890s appears in the fact that none of the original seven was born in the region and that four of them had lived in Minnesota Territory before the area became a state. All seven had been born in the East. On the average they had spent thirty-three years of their lives in Minnesota. Only Du Toit had been educated in the state, having received a common school education in Chaska. None of the seven had any college education; only one had attended an academy (secondary school).

At the time of their appointments, the first seven men came from a variety of occupations. Two were lawyers, two bankers, one a farmer, one a realtor, insurance broker, and grain shipper, and one was a wholesale grocer. With the exception of the lawyers, all had worked in other occupations varying from professional soldier to gold miner. Although they were drawn largely from the generation of the Civil War, only two had been in the military. Only three had any political experience beyond the local level; McHench, Graves, and Corliss had served in the state legislature.

Although none of the appointees had previously tackled a task of this nature, all had some kind of experience that marked them as successful. Lamberton (1831–1905), one of the two Democrats in the original group, had been born in Carlisle, Pennsylvania, had studied law, and had arrived in Minnesota Territory with his wife in 1856. He had acted as city attorney and as mayor of Winona and had helped to organize the Winona Deposit Bank. McHench (1824–95), a New Yorker and the oldest man to sit on the board, was the only farmer. He had settled in Wabasha County in 1856. A Whig who joined the Republican party at its inception, McHench purchased a large tract of land in Martin County in 1879 and served in many local and county offices as well as in the state Senate.[3]

George A. Du Toit (1847–1923) was a country banker—on a statewide basis. In 1870 while operating a drug store in Carver, Minnesota, he founded the Carver County State Bank of Chaska. He shortly disposed of his pharmacy and turned to banking, founding banks in Norwood, Lester Prairie, Belle Plaine, Waconia, Excelsior, Chanhassen, and Augusta. He also was involved in banks in St. Cloud, Duluth, Marshall, and Glencoe and in a lumber company and a wholesale grocery firm. In addition he helped organize and was treasurer of the Minnesota Sugar Company, which helped bring the sugar-beet industry to the state.[4]

If Du Toit was one of the entrepreneurs of the young state, John De Laittre (1832–1912) had one of the more romantic backgrounds. He left his home in Ellsworth, Maine, in 1852 for the California gold fields. In 1865 he settled in Minneapolis where he turned his hand to manufacturing woolens, flour milling, and lumbering. In 1877 he was elected mayor of St. Paul. In 1884 he became president of the Nicollet National Bank and in 1905 of the Farmers and Mechanics Savings Bank. De Laittre was entrusted by the board with the important task of drawing up its contract with the architect.[5]

Charles H. Graves (1839–1928) was the most prominent nationally of all the commissioners. A Massachusetts man, he served with distinction in the Civil War and remained in the army afterward, resigning in 1870 from the Thirty-fourth Infantry Regiment with the rank of colonel. He settled in Duluth and engaged in real estate, insurance, iron mining, and shipping. In 1871 he shipped the first cargo of wheat from Duluth harbor. He served in the state Senate in 1873–76, was mayor of Duluth in 1881, and was speaker of the state House of Representatives in 1889.[6]

The seventh member of the board was Eben E. Corliss (1841–1917) who was born in Vermont and went to Fergus Falls, Minnesota, in 1856 as a lad of fifteen. He served as an infantryman for four years during the Civil War. After the war he studied law, was admitted to the bar, and practiced for thirty-six years in Fergus Falls. He was county attorney of Otter Tail County for a decade. In 1910 he would become custodian of the capitol, a position he held until his death in the statehouse he helped to build.[7]

This was the group of inexperienced public servants who met in the governor's rooms on May 13, 1893. As a first order of business they elected Channing Seabury (1842–1910) vice-president of the board. He was thus given the major responsibility for the group's charge, since the governor was by law the president and an ex officio member. At a time in life when most men are at the peak of their careers (he was fifty-one years of age), Seabury entered upon fourteen years without salary in the service of the state. He was born in Massachusetts, where he attended the local schools and academy at Bridgewater. He left school at the age of fifteen and, after a three-year business apprenticeship in

Wholesale grocer Channing
Seabury, vice-president
and guiding force of the
Board of State Capitol
Commissioners for more
than a decade

New York City, moved to St. Paul in 1860 to carve out a fortune and a name for himself. In 1883, after several kinds of business ventures, he established the wholesale grocery firm of Maxfield & Seabury, which in 1891 became Seabury & Company. In the best New England tradition he contributed his mite to community service. Once when a tornado destroyed the village of Sauk Rapids and again when a forest fire burned the town of Hinckley in 1894, he acted as chairman of the relief committee that rebuilt those towns.[8]

Seabury was a tough-minded, tenacious man in an era of proud self-centered Victorianism. Nothing in his life up to the time of his appointment to the board foreshadowed the kind of aesthetic and political leadership he would render. It was he who directed the board's political strategy through six legislative sessions and five different governors; it was he who patiently dealt with architect Cass Gilbert; it was he who cracked the whip and brought the world-famous painter John La Farge into line. Many of his jousts with the legislature were marked by political infighting. On occasion he rankled his fellow commissioners to the point of loss of friendship. The Minnesota capitol is a visible monument to his persistence, dedication, and skill.

At the first meeting the board moved to advertise for bids for the land on which to build the new capitol. It announced that the bids would be opened on June 28, 1893. Four bids were duly considered. One would merely have added about an acre to the space already in use for the old capitol at Exchange and Wabasha streets. The other three involved lands on the hills above the Mississippi River. Of these, one was an area about two blocks southeast of the present capitol and just north of Central Park (both of which have been absorbed into the present capitol complex). A second was "at the head of Jackson Street" on "Bass Hill" about six blocks northeast of the present capitol. The third was the area bounded by Park Avenue, Cedar Street, and University Avenue, Wabasha Street and Central Avenue. The fourth was in the vicinity of the 1883 capitol. The asking prices for these tracts varied from $175,000 for the lots near the old capitol to $480,000 for the Cedar-Wabasha-Park area. The board decided that the latter was the best site.[9]

At this point the character of the commissioners became apparent. The Cedar-Wabasha-Park area was appropriate, but the price was so unreasonable that these businessmen turned public servants would not accept it. The tract was put together by a combine of seventeen owners; the board decided to attack the combine piecemeal. Twelve of the owners agreed to sell their properties at an appraisal price set by three distinguished citizens, Alexander Ramsey, Henry M. Rice, and Henry S. Fairchild. To avoid collusion, the board also secured two private appraisals. When one of the property owners backed out of the agreement, the board immediately used its power of condemnation. In all, by spending $124.76 for the appraisals, the board secured the site it wanted for a total of $285,225—a saving of $194,775 over the original asking price. The land was occupied by two dwellings and a stable.

Even before the land issue was settled, however, the board undertook its second responsibility—securing a suitable architectural design for the building. In that effort another facet of the character of this remarkable group began to surface. Not only were they astute businessmen determined to get a dollar's value for a dollar spent, they were also skilled politicians. Their activities over the next decade demonstrate that, led by the capable Seabury, they were not merely political opportunists but political strategists of the first order.

If the people of Minnesota were to receive at reasonable cost a building unified in design and unmarred by the changing winds of political expediency, someone must accept responsibility for a strategy to mollify politicians' outcries while maintaining the functional, aesthetic, and economic integrity of the project. The absence of a responsible authority can, and frequently in these United States does, result in a somewhat questionable product.[10] The state of Minnesota was exceedingly fortunate because its Board of State Capitol Commissioners recognized the possibilities and rose to the occasion. The board's handling of the initial design competition is a case in point.

The first indication that anything unusual was afoot came on February 9, 1893. On that day the committee on legislation for the Minnesota chapter of the American Institute of Architects (AIA) unanimously adopted the following resolution for the guidance of the chapter's president, Cass Gilbert, a young St. Paul architect: "Resolved that the Minnesota Chapter of the American Institute of Architects protest against limiting the cost of the new capitol to $2,000,000, as too small a sum to build a building in modern style suitable for the needs of the state."[11]

The new capitol site, looking north toward University Avenue and the Merriam mansion, about 1896

On March 16, 1894, Gilbert wrote to Seabury requesting a meeting, which took place that same evening in Seabury's home. Rapid communication between the two men was easy since Gilbert's office and that of the board were both located in the Endicott Building in St. Paul. There is no record of what took place at the meeting, but we do know that on April 9, 1894, Seabury wrote to the state's attorney general, Henry W. Childs, and asked whether under the law there was any way that the architect selected by the board could be made supervisor of the entire building project and whether the board could increase the stipend of the architect who submitted the winning design. The latter, it was explained, was necessary because the law's requirements for drawings would cost the architect more than the offered stipend would cover. On April 26 the attorney general replied that the fee could not be raised nor could the architect be made superintendent.[12]

On May 29 the board met with a committee from the Minnesota chapter of the AIA, for whom Cass Gilbert was the spokesman. The committee presented four proposals: (1) the project's architect ought to be the superintendent of construction; (2) the architect's pay should be increased from 2½ percent to about 5 percent of the cost of the project; (3) a committee of architects ought to set up rules for the design competition; and (4) a subcommittee of three architects should assist the board's selection committee. These points expressed the dissatisfaction of many of the state's architects with the proposed design competition. Some threatened to boycott it unless the desired changes were made.[13]

On June 5, 1894, the board issued its advertisement for the capitol design competition. "Instructions to Architects" were prepared and distributed, 433 copies in all. The competition was an open one, which any qualified architect was invited to enter. By October 9, 1894, in spite of the architects' threatened boycott, fifty-six sets of drawings had been received. Two architects, Edmund M. Wheelwright of Boston and Henry Ives Cobb of Chicago, were employed as expert advisers to the board and all designs were placed on public display. The board did not have the power to make the changes requested by the AIA committee, and the controversy continued to build. One Duluth architect put the questions quite bluntly to Gilbert: "I wonder why but fifty-six architects competed for the Capitol of this great state when one hundred and eighty-eight competed for far off Washington? Why Messrs Cobb and Wheelwright never compete and why there were so very few prominent names in that list? . . . I find no names of men who have built any of Minnesota's prominent buildings in that list."[14]

The report of advisers Wheelwright and Cobb was received by the board on November 1, 1894, after the controversy had achieved a full head of steam. As a whole, the two experts were not impressed by the fifty-six designs, but they selected the five they considered best. Then they hastened to add that none of them were worthy of the use of granite or any other dressed stone, suggesting that a local limestone be employed and that the building be treated in a "simple, straight-forward manner . . . with no elaborate wood or stucco work, or much, if any, expensive marble work" in the treatment of the interior.[15]

That Gilbert and his professional cohorts had made an impact may be seen in the board's first *Biennial Report* to the governor in 1895. In the work of selecting a design, the *Report* said, "We have been greatly hampered by some of the restrictive provisions of the act." Experience had shown the legislative safeguards to be "unfortunate," and the board had not acted upon the designs received in the competition. "Surely, if we may be left to select a site, without restriction as to its cost,—to choose either granite, brick or sandstone, for the main construction material, at a difference in cost to the state of not less than $300,000 between them,—to use our discretion in the dimensions of the building, etc., it would seem to have been equally safe to have left some of the less important details to the judgment of the board." If you want us to erect a state capitol, the commissioners said in effect, then let us build it. The legislature should guard against overexpenditure of public funds and leave the construction to the board. The report dated January 1, 1895, was followed on January 7 by a letter from Wheelwright, suggesting that a second competition be held and that it be an invited rather than an open one.[16]

Unquestionably, the commissioners were prepared to go to the mat with the legislature over the matter of amending procedures for the design competition. They had the backing of the Minnesota chapter of the AIA and the moral support of their own consulting architects. The board members were willing to accept the responsibility for the project, but they were not willing to have their power restricted by petty legislative hobbles. For once, the artist in America had found a champion.

The first *Biennial Report* contained other grist for the thoughtful legislator. The board had received $10,000 to cover its expenses for the 1893–94 biennium. It had visited and inspected the relatively new capitols of Iowa, Michigan, Indiana, and Connecticut as well as a new courthouse and a federal building in Pittsburgh, Pennsylvania, paid all its operating expenses and the fees of its blue-ribbon appraisers—and had left "unexpended" $1,574.48. Charges of wild spending could not be brought against this group. Following the same kind of parsimonious thinking, the board urged that the law be changed so that the building could be constructed immediately because the depression had lowered the price of materials. For example, structural iron that had cost four to six cents per pound was now selling for one and one-quarter cents. These hard-nosed businessmen with the public's interest at heart went on in a small way to anticipate some of the economic theories of John Maynard Keynes. In times of depression public expenditures should be used to alleviate unemployment, they said. "The far reaching benefits that would accrue to hundreds of our fellow citizens, not alone upon the building itself, but in the stone quarries, brick kilns, iron foundries, etc., within our state, are easily apparent."[17]

The board's request for changes in the law relating to its powers, the architect's position, and the competition for design were put into proper form and duly introduced into both houses of the legislature in 1895. With only a few inconsequential changes the House granted its approval. The Senate then turned to its version of the bill, which was sponsored by Senator Hiram F. Stevens of Ramsey County. Two changes dealt with the competition. The first eliminated the number of drawings an architect would be required to submit in any competition; the second altered minor details governing the board's management of the competition. Two other changes were broader in scope, empowering the board to discharge an architect whose work might prove unsatisfactory and striking out the clause limiting the architect's fee to 2½ percent. In short, the bill would give the architects the very things they had outlined in their May 1894 meeting with the board. And it would give the board the power it had requested in its first report to the governor. The one item not provided was a financing plan that would permit the commissioners to take advantage of the depressed condition of the economy.[18]

The first three changes were accepted without comment, but the removal of a limit on the architect's fee caused no little debate. After all, said one senator, in the face of the declining wage rates for the workingman, it was only fair for the professional class to give up something graciously; 2½ percent of the cost of a project as big as this ought to be enough money for any man. The Senate finally accepted a compromise; the state would pay a fee of 5 percent of the first $500,000, 4 percent of the second $500,000, and 3 percent of the remainder. The bill passed easily by a vote of 41 to 12. Two days later on March 9, Governor David M. Clough signed it into law. In this exercise in legislative politics the Board of State Capitol Commissioners, assisted by the Minnesota chapter of the AIA, had done its homework well. In March 1895 the strategy dimly perceivable in the wording of the architects' proposals of May 1894 was a successful reality.[19]

On April 11 the board tidied up the loose ends by rejecting all the designs submitted in the first competition. On April 15 it began to advertise the details of a second competition. The second set of "Instructions for Architects" contained one omission that would become important; it did not specify that the capitol be built of Minnesota stone. Hindsight permits us to realize that another phase of the board's strategy was in the making, and this time it would deal with aesthetics.[20]

By August 5, 1895, forty-one designs had been submitted. Wheelwright, who was again employed as consultant, commended them in his report on October 17. "The average merit of these designs," he commented, "was much higher than the previous competition, and the plans of the five designs which I recommend for premiums are, in their adaptation to the special needs of this building, superior to the best plan presented in the former competition." The five designs recommended for premiums were those of George R. Mann of St. Louis; Wendell & Humphreys of Denver; Bassford, Traphagen & Fitzpatrick of St. Paul and Duluth; Cass Gilbert of St. Paul; and Clarence H. Johnston of St. Paul. The order was not indicative of preference.[21]

Eight days later the board began its deliberations by casting informal ballots. For the next two days the design of Bassford, Traphagen & Fitzpatrick consistently led the field but just as consistently failed to receive a majority of the votes cast. Cass Gilbert's design did not achieve a plurality on any ballot, and on four of the seven it got only one vote. When the group reconvened on October 30, Seabury persuaded the commissioners to abandon their effort to decide the winning architect by ballot. He then moved, and Daniel Shell seconded, the following motion: "Resolved: That this Board, having carefully examined all of the designs submitted in this (second) competition, and having been thoroughly advised with respect to each of them, hereby makes the following awards." Then followed the names in order of their ranking: Cass Gilbert, George Mann, Bassford, Traphagen & Fitzpatrick, Clarence H. Johnston, and Harry W. Jones.[22]

The deed was done. Minnesota's new capitol would be designed and its construction supervised by a St. Paul architect. Gilbert, in a draft of the covering letter for his design, dated September 9, 1895, had outlined the factors he believed important: "The first elements considered in making this design," he wrote, "have been the practical ones of *economy* and good *construction*. Next after this, and hardly less important have been the questions of a suitable and convenient arrangement of the interior of the building giving ample light and ventilation to all its parts, and convenient access between those parts of the

The fifth-place design by Harry W. Jones of Minneapolis

St. Paul architect Clarence H. Johnston's fourth-place design

The third-place design by architects Bassford, Traphagen, and Fitzpatrick of St. Paul and Duluth

The second-place design by George R. Mann of St. Louis

structure most requiring it. And, finally, that it shall express in all its parts and as a whole the nature of the building and the dignity of its purpose."[23]

In a section of the letter headed "Materials to be Used," Gilbert wrote that they "are to be the best of their respective kinds. The entire exterior up to the spring of the dome will be of Granite or Montana marble [or] Kettle River Sandstone or a combination of both. The bell of the dome would be of white marble if contract estimates will allow of such expense, otherwise of heavy cast iron either gilded or painted white, as in many of the notable domes of the world. . . . The granite or marble work includes the columns, cornices, and balustrades and ornamental work shown on elevations. The sculpture should be of marble."[24]

Cass Gilbert's winning design for the capitol as it appeared in 1898 (with minor changes from 1895)

Gilbert's design suggested that the building would have a graceful eclectic style derived from the architecture of sixteenth-century Italy surmounted by a modern engineering version of the dome of St. Peter's Basilica in Rome. It would be fireproof; it would incorporate the latest features in climate control and lighting. It would, in short, provide for the space needs, the protection of records, the health of employees, and the pride of the citizens of the state. The design was governed by a decided sense of functionalism, but the idea of a simple structure in which to conduct the business of the state was elevated into a dramatic edifice that in itself would express dignity and power. Gilbert's capitol was everything the legislature had asked for and more—how much more neither the legislature nor the public could yet know.

The public's immediate response to Gilbert's design was generally favorable. The *St. Paul Dispatch* exulted in the victory of a city architect. The *Minneapolis Tribune* was sorry that a Minneapolis man had not won, but "glad that it went to a Minnesota man." The *St. Paul Pioneer Press* praised the board's selection and devoted half a column to extolling the superiority of western architects over eastern ones, commenting that Gilbert's design reflected a severe simplicity "whose strength lies in the symmetry of its proportions and the subordination of all ideas of ornamental detail to the general effect of the mass."[25]

In the one note of sour grapes in the whole affair, the *Minneapolis Journal* of October 31 said, "The award to Cass Gilbert is in accordance with a prophecy in The Journal a year or more ago, when it was said that the first competition was to be thrown out in order to let in Cass Gilbert of St. Paul, who was slated for the first place and the supervision of the building. Mr. Gilbert is a connection, by marriage, of Mr. Seabury, of the commission, and it has been understood ever since The Journal's publication just referred to, that he was to have the plum."[26] The *Journal* would not, until forced to do so, moderate its criticism of the project. It was apparently the only metropolitan newspaper to hold such negative views.

But it was not alone in suspecting that something might be amiss. The Denver architectural firm of Wendell & Humphreys complained that "politics" had influenced the awards. The board at its December 17 meeting decided that "the letter of Mess. Wendell & Humphries [*sic*] be returned to them by the Vice President, with the statement that the Board considers their insinuation that local politics influenced the award of premiums, were uncalled for, and that the Board does not care to file such communications." In its second report the board felt the need to notice these accusations, for it asserted that the selection was in accordance with the opinion of Wheelwright. No other documents supporting this statement have come to light. Perhaps it was a verbal opinion that historians are unable to recall from the winds.[27]

Harry W. Jones, a Minneapolis architect, seems to have had the last word in the *Minneapolis Journal* of October 31, 1895. "I am very much pleased that Mr. Gilbert was given the capitol award," he said. "It was my personal opinion some time ago that his designs were entitled to the first place and I have no sympathy with the talk that I hear on the streets to the effect that the award was in any way biased. It is very fortunate for the state that the plans of an architect of Mr. Gilbert's standing were selected. He represents the progressive, educated class of architects, the class which is everywhere getting to the front nowadays. We have, in the building of a capitol, to consider not only today, but the future, and it would have been very unfortunate to have had plans selected which did not represent the best of modern thought in an architectural way."

Cass Gilbert (seated) and his staff with capitol floor plan, about 1900

2 · The Architect

CASS GILBERT was just twenty-five days short of his thirty-sixth birthday when he received the design award for the Minnesota State Capitol in 1895. He had been born on November 24, 1859, in Zanesville, Ohio, the birthplace sixteen years later of America's popular western novelist, Zane Grey. His parents, Colonel Samuel A. and Elizabeth F. (Wheeler) Gilbert, moved to St. Paul shortly after the Civil War. After his father's sudden death, his mother raised Cass and his two brothers on Samuel's Civil War pension and income from a few real estate holdings. Cass spent several summers in the countryside, worked for a carpenter in Red Wing, and briefly attended the forerunner to Macalester College. In 1876, at age sixteen, he became a draftsman's apprentice in the office of the St. Paul architect Abraham Radcliffe, where his boyhood friend, Clarence Johnston, already worked.[1]

Gilbert's formal training in the art of building was rather extensive for his era. In 1878–79 he and Johnston moved to Boston to study architecture at the Massachusetts Institute of Technology. After about a year of traveling in England, France, and Italy, Gilbert entered the office of McKim, Mead and White as a draftsman. This New York City firm of architects was on its way to becoming the most prominent in the United States. In 1881 his employers sent him to St. Paul to take charge of some work there. In December of the next year he opened an office in St. Paul in partnership with James Knox Taylor. The firm was unable to support two men, so Taylor withdrew. Even so, Gilbert, who had married Julia T. Finch on November 29, 1887, made his living with a few commissions from architecture and a rather steady sale of watercolors "at which he was very proficient."

In March 1893, when the matter of a new state capitol was nearing initial legislative acceptance, Gilbert wangled an appointment with Governor Knute Nelson through a letter of introduction from Joseph A. Wheelock, editor of the

St. Paul Pioneer Press. As Wheelock outlined Gilbert's accomplishments: "He is the Superintendent of the new Custom House and Post Office to be built in this City. What Architects think of his qualifications is shown by the fact that he has been recently appointed one of the Board of Judges of Architecture, at the [Chicago] World's Fair."[2]

The World's Columbian Exposition, which opened May 1, 1893, in Chicago was the largest fair the United States had seen. Gilbert's connection with that undertaking enhanced his reputation. He was willing to trade on that connection as well as his association with a prestigious firm. In the latter case, he told the board in 1895 that he was "authorized by Messers. McKim, Mead & White of New York to state that I may count upon them as consulting architects should the Board desire." As Wayne Andrews has written, "all great architects have been poets, [and] the very greatest have had to double as salesmen in order to survive."[3]

Gilbert's design for the Minnesota capitol, conceived "along lines considered historically appropriate for public work," was his first big break. On the strength of that project he would move his office to New York City in 1899 and embark on a successful career in ecclesiastical, scholastic, business, and government architecture that brought him many high honors.[4]

Architect Frank Lloyd Wright once wrote that Gilbert and others like him were "merely useful tools of this devastating power" of "trade and machine production [that] are having their way and their say in the standardizations of our day."[5] Nevertheless, Gilbert's lifework represents something richer and more human than the sterile products of steel, glass, and shiny plastic that often result from the power of "trade and machine production." Cass Gilbert's Minnesota capitol was not designed with modern values in mind. He did not set out to provide merely creature comforts (though he did place toilets on every floor) nor did he try only to enhance employee efficiency (though there was a convenience factor in the space assignments). Rather he attempted to express in the building's form an ideal that would excite the spirit and the dreams of a people.

Egerton Swartwout, whose biographical sketch of Gilbert is based in part upon personal recollections, draws a picture of Gilbert as a hard-working, honest, Victorian gentleman who was a stickler for details and whose values were depicted in his paintings and his buildings. He was, Swartwout wrote, "purposely impressive in manner and rather pompous at times. . . . He was a good salesman, and although he won a few competitions, the bulk of his work came from past performances plus his unique ability to convince his prospective clients. He was impressive and could handle his clients well, especially at first, but he was not always tactful and sometimes held to his position too firmly. He liked to have his own way in everything he undertook; he had convictions and expressed them strongly, a fact that undoubtedly affected his popularity among many with whom he came into contact."[6]

The contract between Gilbert and the board demonstrates something of the character of the man.[7] In it the board included an article to the effect that Gilbert would "supervise the construction, erection, finishing and furnishing entire and complete the said State Capitol building," to which Gilbert added "including the embellishment of the grounds constituting the site of said State Capitol." He wanted it plainly understood that he conceived of the project as a unified whole and that he would direct it down to the last blade of grass. The board was his client, but the building was Cass Gilbert's brain child; he would care for it. The relationship between client and architect was made even clearer in the matter of the power of the building superintendent. The board specified that it would employ such an agent to "assist" the architect "in supervising and inspecting the work. Said superintendent shall be subject to the direction and control of said Board of Capitol Commissioners." Gilbert added, "But said Superintendent shall have no power or authority to change or modify the plans, drawings or specifications of . . . [the architect], nor to issue any order or orders contravening the directions of said . . . [architect] as to the conduct of said work, and he shall be dismissed upon the request of the . . . [architect] for any reasonable ground, incompetency or bad faith." In other words, the client's interests were to be protected, but those interests were limited to getting full value for each dollar spent and they were not in any way to interfere with the architect's power to direct the work. To the board of tough-minded businessmen it should have been unmistakably clear from the very beginning of their association with Gilbert that he was indeed, as Swartwout said, a man of "strong convictions" who "liked to have his own way in everything he undertook."

According to his official reports, Gilbert's activities were quite straightforward. He began reducing his design sketches to preliminary drawings which the board could amend and revise, then he prepared the working drawings that would guide the construction contractors.[8] His report gave no hint of anything more than daily routine, but other evidence suggests that many things—perhaps anticipated only by the architect—were in the works.

About the same time that Gilbert was selected to design Minnesota's capitol, a group of artists who specialized in decorating walls with paintings formed the National Society of Mural Painters. One of the reasons for the association was to "establish an educational propaganda" campaign to persuade architects and commissioners for public buildings to adorn the interiors of the structures with paintings. While the art of mural painting was a very old one and its practitioners read like a roll call of the great Italian painters of the fifteenth and sixteenth centuries—Michelangelo, Leonardo da Vinci, Raphael, among others—America, with its Puritan distrust of excesses and its plain style of business in the age of democracy, had not been a fertile ground for murals. Although a few homes of the rich were so decorated in the nineteenth century, it was not until 1876, when architect Henry H. Richardson employed John La Farge to decorate Trinity Church in Boston, that modern mural painting had much impact in the United States.[9]

When sometime water colorist Cass Gilbert began thinking about his first monumental assignment, the mural painters society was just beginning its "educational propaganda" campaign. Who opened the exchange between Gilbert and the group is not clear, but early in 1896 the architect was in communication with the society. A letter from the corresponding secretary expressed sympathy for Gilbert's difficulties in finding the money to put murals in his new building. "The Society understands the difficulties at the present time in having any committee on a public building appreciate its artistic opportunities," the corresponding secretary wrote, "and are very much in sympathy with the architect in any endeavor of his to secure the proper recognition of the 'arts decorative' in connection with the constructional questions." The society would, the letter promised, write to the Board of State Capitol Commissioners and encourage it to "facilitate affirmative action in this direction." Whether the idea of murals in the new building was Gilbert's or the society's, another concept had entered the picture and an expensive one at that.[10]

Gilbert's edificial symbol of the state was also creating ripples throughout Minnesota. The activities of one William C. Baxter of Minneapolis can serve as an example. He had for some time been engaged in granite quarrying in the Ortonville–Bellingham area, taking out stone for monuments. In the spring of 1896 he began maneuvering to move his operations to the St. Cloud–Rockville–Cold Spring region by opening negotiations for the purchase of the Samuel T. Doyle quarries near St. Cloud. As Baxter told the local newspaper, Gilbert's design for the state capitol "necessitated the use of light colored stone" and the "grey granite . . . [in central Minnesota] was the lightest [colored] article in the state." The St. Cloud Businessmen's Association was delighted with his idea and saw to it that the city council gave its best efforts to ease the financial burden of Baxter's move to that city.[11]

When the metropolitan newspapers reported that Commissioner Henry W. Lamberton of Winona had said that the board was seriously considering the use of Winona limestone for the foundations of the new capitol, the *St. Cloud Daily Times* of April 30, 1896, voiced decided objections to that material: "A prominent St. Cloud stonecutter who was employed on the Chicago City Hall and court house says that it is already showing signs of decay. . . . It is likely that the [lime]stone would last long enough so that the present commission would never discover the mistake but the capitol is expected to stand longer than one generation."

An architect can, in the shelter of his expertise, ignore such attempts to make policy in the streets, but when his employer begins writing him letters, it is a different matter. It takes time to train a client to his role, and Gilbert was bound to listen when Commissioner De Laittre wrote him a note suggesting changes in the specifications on some of the foundation work to economize on but not to "cheapen" the building. Probably as a result of De Laittre's suggestion, the contract for grading, excavation, and foundation work awarded to George J. Grant of St. Paul on April 30, 1896, called for the use of other types of stone as well as granite. It specified that "the bearing blocks are to be of granite, the area walls and step foundations of local blue limestone, the dome foundations of Kettle River sandstone and all other walls and piers to be of Winona or Kettle River sandstone."[12]

In the midst of the hubbub, ground-breaking ceremonies were held on May 6, 1896, and it was time for the "working stiffs" like Joseph Shiely, Sr.—a stone cutter who in 1914 would found a building materials contracting firm, the J. L. Shiely Company of St. Paul—to begin fitting stone on stone.[13] At this point the dream began taking shape as reality.

Grant completed work on the excavation and foundations on December 5, 1896. Meanwhile, in September the contract for the structural iron and steel for the basement floor was let to the Universal Construction Company of Chicago. Two days after Grant finished his work, Universal Construction began. In less than a month the job was completed. Minnesota had a fine new foundation and a steel frame for a basement floor (above the subbasement). And the board had run out of money.[14]

Appropriations from 1893 to 1897 produced $382,707.73. The board's operating expenses (including $5,160.87 for the per diem and traveling expenses of the commissioners for three years and eight months and $159.00 for stationery and postage), payments for the site, materials, and construction came to $382,274.46, leaving a balance for use in the 1897 construction season of $433.27.[15] The pay-as-you-go system anticipated by the 1891 legislature was proving to be more "stop" than "go." It was time for another bit of legislative politicking; again the initiative passed into the hands of Channing Seabury.

Seabury asked Gilbert to outline the work that *"could* be done, if we had sufficient funds, during 1897 and 1898." Then he began collecting documentation from uninvolved architects, the State Board of Health, and the governor's office relating to the need for haste in completing the task at hand. Gilbert dutifully included in his annual report to the board a number of letters from reliable contractors who offered their predictions concerning wage and material costs in the future—everyone expected them to rise. And, he said, it is necessary to give contractors sufficient lead time for calculation and preparation. "This is especially the case," wrote Gilbert, "in the stone work, where the stone should be allowed to season for a certain length of time after it is quarried, and before it is placed in the building, in order that any defects in the material may become apparent and the imperfect stone be rejected."[16]

Seabury carefully prepared his case for improved funding; the board's second *Biennial Report* in 1897 was a fine document for developing political pressure. The vice-president detailed the work that had been done and recorded the appointments of Frank E. Hanson of St. Paul as secretary of the board and John Boland of Minneapolis as superintendent of construction. He also noted that "during the winter of 1895–96 our board invited all the different quarry men throughout this state to submit samples of their several products, uniform in size and cutting, in order that they might be erected upon the site,

Channing Seabury wields the first shovel of dirt at groundbreaking ceremonies, May 6, 1896

for exposure to the elements, comparison, etc. . . . an interesting series of these sample stones may be seen near the Wabasha street front of the site. It is our purpose to test the qualities, liability to discoloration, etc., of these various stones in this way before selecting the material for the superstructure of the building." There was to be no favoritism in the selection of materials; everyone

Quarried stone, perhaps Georgia marble, ready to be shipped to St. Paul

in town could check the samples for himself. Seabury went on to say that the cost of the project was thus far staying well below estimates; the iron and steel work in the basement floor had been completed at nearly 30 percent below the estimate. Happily, all was proceeding better than anyone had a right to expect.[17]

Nevertheless, the picture was a gloomy one. Property valuations in the state, contrary to the expectations of the 1893 legislature, were declining, and the receipts for funding construction work in 1897 were actually less than for 1896. Exhaustion of funds had prevented the purchase of all the iron and steel needed for the building at the current low prices. At the same time, wages were low; stonecutters were receiving only $3.00 a day, compared to the earlier wage of $4.00, bricklayers were getting $3.50, and common laborers were receiving only $1.25. Now was the time to go ahead, but the board's hands were tied.[18]

"Our board now finds itself at a point where valuable time will be lost," warned Seabury. "We are ready to advertise for . . . a contract for the erection of the superstructure of the building. This work ought to follow closely upon that already done, otherwise the elements will damage the excellent foundation now in place. Material, of all kinds, is exceptionally low in price. Men have long been idle and greatly need employment. . . . but we are unable to take advantage of the facts stated, because we have no more funds available for building purposes, and we are prohibited, by the act of 1893, from making any contracts that bind the state to payment earlier than the same are available under the act." The document was a patient restatement of all the earlier arguments in the current context with a careful notation of facts and figures published for all to see. Give us the authority, the report says again, and we will put up your capitol. "No private citizen," the report pointed out, "constructs buildings in the halting, dilatory and wasteful way that these public buildings are usually handled. We should be glad to make an exception of this one, and to push it forward to completion and early occupancy."[19]

The *Journals* of the legislature for 1897 suggest that so surely was the pressure developed and applied that a race ensued to see which chamber could be the first to give the board permission to get on with the job. House File 625, introduced by the Ramsey County delegation on February 25 (as was Senate File 364), won the race, became a substitute bill for Senate File 364, and was signed by the governor on April 3, 1897.[20] This law granted the Board of State Capitol Commissioners the authority to issue up to $500,000 worth of certificates of indebtedness for the completion of the new capitol. Seemingly nothing stood in the way of getting the whole project speedily completed, perhaps as early as 1903.

A *Minneapolis Journal* cartoon suggesting the angry debate preceding the selection of white Georgia marble for the capitol superstructure

3 · The Politics of Public Architecture

THE DELAY in the progress of the capitol caused by the shortage of cash funds during the winter of 1897 was the last lengthy slowdown on the project. Armed with the power of credit the Board of State Capitol Commissioners was in a position to "drive," to use one of Vice-president Seabury's favorite words. With this vote of confidence from the legislature, the commissioners turned to *the* important decision: letting the contract for the superstructure of the building. The importance of the decision weighed heavily on them, because it would be the principal factor in both the cost and the appearance of the final structure. Lurking in the background was a political element that could, if not treated with respect, result in at least a short-run loss of popularity for the board. If it swelled to greater proportions, it might bring about the dismissal of the commissioners and the appointment of new ones. That would mean unconscionable delay, perhaps a new architect, and a building that would probably lack the aesthetic unity the commissioners hoped for. They approached the decision on tenterhooks.

Gilbert seems not to have suffered the same qualms. On April 9, 1897, six days after the board had been granted the power to issue certificates of indebtedness, the architect reported that his drawings were "sufficiently advanced to permit the letting of a contract at an early date." He was immediately told to slow down; he was asked to prepare a series of specifications that would permit separate bids for the various parts of the building (exterior and roof, interior, dome, steel and iron work), for alternative methods of construction, and for such various materials as the contractors "might wish to offer." It is probable that the commissioners were not fully aware of the far-reaching implications of this directive. The first part of it—to construct the various segments of the building on separate contracts—made possible decisions on the dome and the interior in a climate of opinion that allowed for elaborations no one would have dared to contemplate immediately after the depression of 1893. The board, however, was very conscious of the postdepression psychology of the citizens and intended to ensure strict economy. Gilbert, firm-minded man that he was, disliked the directive allowing the contractors a choice of materials. He wanted to control everything that went into the building, and he had said so—quite plainly. But the board would not back down. It "desired to give all bidders and the various materials in the market an equal chance, and provided accordingly." Architects will manipulate clients when they can; when they cannot, they usually give way graciously.[1]

In the middle of June the board opened the fourteen bids that had been received on the construction of the exterior and the roof. The commissioners then found themselves unable or unwilling to decide, so they instructed the architect to prepare a report on the bids and to seek ways to reduce the cost. For the next two months Gilbert very definitely held the "butt end" of the problem, as John De Laittre put it.[2]

In the midst of this imbroglio, Gilbert received a letter from Lucian Swift, manager and part owner of the *Minneapolis Journal,* which would have important consequences later in the year and would show a seldom revealed side of the architect's character. The letter from Swift was short and to the point: "As I am personally interested in the Minnesota Sand Stone Company I naturally desire that they should obtain some work from the capitol building," Swift wrote. "I suppose that you are posted in regard to this stone so it is unnecessary for me to enter into any details as regards its merit, but if possible I would like to have you post me as to anything I might do in order to push its merits with the commissioners. The company of course does not intend to figure on doing any building, but would like to furnish the contractors with the stone. If you could give me any pointers, or do anything for us in this line, it would be appreciated." The letter was not unusual; Gilbert received many similar appeals from various people. We do not know what he said in reply, but his office stamp indicates that he answered Swift on June 14. Not until September would he become aware of the letter's potential usefulness; then he would move with dispatch.[3]

At about the same time, the commissioners were beginning to speak up to him, and signs of a split in the board's support of its architect began to appear. Graves, the commissioner from the Sixth Congressional District, was very sensitive about two things: that the board must not exceed the legislative limits on the total cost of the project and that his central Minnesota district was an important source of excellent granite. The first factor was preying on his mind when he wrote to Seabury in June 1897: "I feel obliged to insist that Friend Gilbert, who is all right from his standpoint, must radically change his specifications for

Gov. John Lind, PRESIDENT (EX OFFICIO)

CHANNING SEABURY, VICE PRES.

E. E. CORLISS, JOHN DE LAITTRE, G. A. DU TOIT, C. H. GRAVES, H. W. LAMBERTON, EDGAR WEAVER, COMMISSIONERS

FRANK E. HANSON, SECRETARY

Board of STATE CAPITOL Commissioners.

St. Paul, Minn. Nov. 25, 1899.

NOV 28 1899 ANS. 111-5th AVE., NEW YORK CITY.

My Dear Cass:-

I have just come from the Capitol, where I have spent about two and a half hours wandering about. The weather has been perfect ever since you left, and just about the same temperature as it was the week you were home, consequently, they have been laying Marble and brick without interruption. The front entrance now looks exactly like the three others; the main walls being up to an even line, all around the building, while none of the capitals are in place on the columns in the Logias. They have today hauled the four that belong on the west end, and two of them have been elevated on to the walls, but are not yet in place. Joe says that if they have three or four days more of this mild weather, (which promises to continue,) they will have completed the small amount of this Marble work which remains to be done.

They have made a good start on the roof trusses, over the north pavilion, four of them being in place this afternoon, and this branch of the work begins to make quite a showing over the House of Representatives.

All the Kettle River stone, which is on the grounds, has been erected on the dome piers, and Joe told me that probably four cars had arrived today, which he hoped to set next week, weather permitting.

One of Commissioner Seabury's many detailed letters to Cass Gilbert, 1899

those for a building unlimited in cost to those for a building of the class for which the Legislature has made appropriation, and that is, a fire proof building, strongly built, but with not a dollar unnecessarily expended."[4]

At any rate, Gilbert's report on the bids was submitted on July 8, and the board advertised for new bids for the general construction of all but the dome and the interior. It also asked for bids on the drainage system and the concrete floor of the subbasement. Gilbert used the next month to prepare his case in the matter of the contractors' choices of materials. He sent samples of the stones to Professor William O. Crosby of the Massachusetts Institute of Technology and dug out reports on various kinds of stone from federal government engineers, the Smithsonian Institution, and the United States Geological Survey. With these he built his arguments for the board meeting of August 19.[5]

After a careful analysis of the cost factors in the bids, Gilbert's report turned to the matter (if we accept the number of words devoted to the topic as evidence) that was nearest his heart. The materials in the bids ranged over a good share of the kinds of building stone available in the states east of the Mississippi River. Several bidders offered the possibility of using two varieties of stone. Gilbert quickly dismissed the idea of using one type of stone for the first story and finishing off the structure with another. It would, he said, "ruin the appearance of the building." He preferred to use only one kind of stone in the whole structure. His reports from experts, he stated, showed that any of the suggested materials would be structurally sound, but there was the important consideration of aesthetic quality. "It is essential that a building of such proportions should be constructed of material of light color. The use of a dark color would inevitably make the building appear gloomy and forbidding," he wrote.

"While a number of kinds of stone offered fill some of these conditions, I do not find that any of them fill the conditions so fully as Georgia Marble. Its beautiful color, its brilliant crystalline structure, its facility in working, its strength under pressure, its durability in exposure to the atmosphere, and the immense quantities available, together with the moderate cost, make it in my opinion the most desirable material."

The possibility of using marble had never entered his head, he continued, until he investigated the contractors' bids. "In submitting my original competitive designs for the building," he said piously, "as will appear by the specifications and letter accompanying the same, I did not contemplate the use of marble, believing that its cost would be beyond the limit of the appropriation." (We should not recall too loudly the draft of his covering letter in September 1895.)[6] His conclusions were based, he implied, on the pure considerations of aesthetics, strength, and economy. In no way was he trying to force his opinion on the board; he was their servant. He concluded his report by suggesting that if a combination of materials were to be adopted he would "recommend St. Cloud, Rockville or Little Falls Granite for the Basement, and Georgia Marble for the walls above the Basement." In short, if politics *were* to enter into the decision, this compromise would be acceptable to him. It would seem that Cass Gilbert was demonstrating, in the sequence of events outlined here, some of that skill in dealing with a client for which he became notorious. Now the board had its expert's advice and was prepared to move—if it could get up the courage.

The subbasement matter was easily handled; on August 19 the contract was awarded to Lauer Bros. & Miller of St. Paul. (That company would complete its work on October 12 "at a cost slightly less than the original contract.")[7] To all intents and purposes, the state owned a completed foundation that imposed certain limits in size, shape, and outline, but beyond that point the superstructure could be developed in a variety of ways.

The board met almost daily from August 10 to 31, 1897. The struggle centered on three points: the politics of public architecture, cost, and aesthetics. The politics of public architecture held that the expenditure of tax money for the construction of public buildings ought to bring the maximum profit to the citizens of the state; hence local materials should be used whenever possible. The legislature, however, had imposed an exact limit on the costs of the capitol, and many people, on the board and otherwise, were aware that Minnesota granite—the most plentiful and the most imposing local material—was very expensive because it was so difficult to prepare.

In the matter of aesthetics two factors were relevant: tradition in both the United States and Europe maintained that marble was the only suitable material for monumental public works; all the Minnesota construction stone (granite, sandstone, and limestone—with the possible exception of Winona limestone) was dark in color and would result in a structure that would glower down on the city. Day after day the seven men argued, voted, disagreed, started over, questioned their architect, pored over the reports, asked for more information, and delayed.

The pressure to use Minnesota stone must have been tremendous. Of the 24 bids listed by the architect in his report to the board, which ranged from $474,400 for Bedford limestone to $1,055,614 for Troy White Granite, 12 bids were lower than that finally accepted. Of those 12 low bids, all but four were for stone from outside the state, which apparently received little consideration. The four low bids involving Minnesota materials used either Kettle River sandstone or Winona limestone. The report of Professor Crosby on his tests of these stones indicated that Kettle River sandstone crumbled badly in the fire test and that Winona limestone might "be used with confidence in all but the most exposed and moist situations." The five bids involving Minnesota's most famous building stone, granite, ranged from William C. Baxter's bid of $737,000 for St. Cloud granite to $950,000 for Little Falls granite.[8]

On the last day of August the board went into executive session. The entire morning was consumed by a full statement from each commissioner of his opinion on the question. In the afternoon, with Governor Clough in attendance, the commissioners continued their statements. The governor must have felt that it was time to bite the bullet. The minutes of the meeting recorded that he "expressed himself as being firmly in favor of using Minnesota stone, and hoped that the Board would adopt Minnesota material, at the same time expressing no preference. He also stated that so long as he should be Governor of the State he would never approve a voucher which should make the total cost of the building exceed the appropriation."[9]

Crew at Biesanz quarry in Winona, which produced stone for the capitol foundation, about 1900

It must have been a weary group of men who returned to the interminable chore of balloting. A motion to build the superstructure of St. Cloud granite was voted down four to three with De Laittre, Du Toit, and Weaver voting in favor and Corliss, Graves, Lamberton, and Seabury voting nay. The proposition to build the entire superstructure of Georgia marble lost four to three with Corliss, Du Toit, Graves, and Weaver against and De Laittre, Lamberton, and Seabury for. At last a motion to build the basement of St. Cloud granite, the superstructure of Georgia marble, and the dome foundation and piers of Kettle River sandstone was adopted, with De Laittre, Graves, Lamberton, and Seabury voting aye, and Corliss, Du Toit, and Weaver voting nay. The bid of $690,000 submitted by St. Paul's Butler-Ryan Company—which was $47,000 less than the lowest Minnesota granite bid—was accepted. The decision was made, though the board would never be the same again. The only step remaining was to award the contract.[10]

It seemed so simple; it was not. The board's choice of Georgia marble brought on the political storm the commissioners had feared. The invective of nineteenth-century journalism and the economic chauvinism of the turn of the century spewed across the pages of the state's newspapers. The *St. Cloud Daily Times* of September 1, 1897, reported that Simeon A. Jones, a granite producer of that city, had learned (incorrectly, as matters turned out) that such granite as would be used would be quarried in Stearns County but dressed in St. Paul, which meant that only about one-sixth of the money spent on granite would remain in St. Cloud.

Such news was more than enough to make a country editor swing from the heels; editor and proprietor Colin F. Macdonald of the *St. Cloud Daily Times* did just that. The very next day he fired

Quarry site, probably near St. Cloud, one center of the state's granite industry, about 1900

his first editorial cannonade: "No Berkshire swine ever exceeded in ravenous greed the denizens of St. Paul. . . . The decision of the commission . . . is all in the interest of St. Paul. . . . With marble . . . practically all the labor will be employed in St. Paul. . . . she has already 'cabbaged' nearly one-sixth of the $2,000,000 for unsalable real estate, and has made arrangements by which at least $1,300,000 of the balance will be disbursed in St. Paul." Not satisfied with flaying St. Paulites, the editor published an ominous warning for Sixth District Commissioner Graves. He had tried for Congress once, wrote Macdonald, and probably would again. When he did, "he should be told to go to Georgia for his votes, where he went to get stone for Minnesota's Capitol. Remember Graves!"

In its news columns on September 2, 1897, the *Daily Times* reprinted an editorial from the *Minneapolis Journal* in which that newspaper—the only metropolitan journal to oppose the decision—said that the marble was a slap in the face for the "reputation of Minnesota building stone." The marble may be more handsome "and possibly add something to the value of real estate in St. Paul, but it certainly is not adding much to the interests of the state to have it [the capitol] surfaced with outside stone." Even the *Journal,* however, felt that the cost of a granite structure might exceed the limitations set by the 1893 legislature.

When the *St. Paul Pioneer Press* of September 3, 1897, asked what editor Macdonald knew about the architectural or artistic requirements of the design adopted for the new capitol, that doughty Scotsman shot back on the same day: "A damned sight more than the chattel-mortgaged *Pioneer Press.* . . . Of what benefit," Macdonald asked, "is it to the granite centers that their material is put in the foundation, the usual place for inferior materials, and where but little of it can be seen, or will ever attract attention? And all this because the architect, an enemy of Minnesota stone, regarded marble as *prettier* to look at."[11]

The *St. Cloud Daily Times* continued to reprint the editorials of its metropolitan supporter, the *Minneapolis Journal,* which produced a new scapegoat. The blame should be put on Governor Clough, editorialized the *Journal,* because he told the commissioners that the cost of a granite superstructure would exceed the limits set by the legislature and that he would refuse payment for any contract specifying granite. "The governor thus put the knife to the hilt in the heart of the granite men," said the *Daily Times* of September 6, 1897.

Macdonald also found support in most of the local newspapers around him; all of central Minnesota seemed to be up in arms. He gleaned a populist bomb from the *Elk River Star News:* "It was practically the unanimous wish of the common people that the new Capitol be built of Minnesota stone, but a majority of the commission have seen fit to ignore this wish." From the *Alexandria Post News* Macdonald reprinted the notion that the decision was a "direct insult." The *Little Falls Herald* stated that "the people of the state will strongly disapprove." The *Sauk Rapids Sentinel* articulated the threat most feared by the board when it called for "mass meetings" to "protest against building the Capitol at this time."[12]

The political storm seemed to be building around the commissioners, but how much of it was tornadic and how much *flatus ventris de vox populi* is difficult to determine. The position of the St. Cloud editor was probably representative of many citizens. A new public building is seldom viewed as an architectural problem whose limits are determined by taste; more often it is regarded primarily as an economic opportunity, a generator of jobs for the community the building is to serve. This attitude was so powerful in the case of the capitol that the St. Cloud attack on one of the perpetrators of the "foul deed" went beyond words in the public print. By 1899 Seabury reported to the state senator from

Stearns County that St. Cloud merchants were taking their revenge on him by boycotting his wholesale grocery firm.[13]

If one is to judge by the gubernatorial race of 1898, however, the political effects of the capitol windstorm were hard to find. The five central Minnesota counties (Stearns, Benton, Douglas, Meeker, and Sherburne) gave 60 percent of the vote to the Democrat, John Lind—not much different from two of the other three elections in the 1890s. Only in 1894, when the popular Knute Nelson ran for his second term, did the Republican candidate outpoll the Democrat in the central area. Nevertheless, the feeling among the people responsible for the capitol project was that the heat in the kitchen was becoming unbearably hot.[14]

At this point Cass Gilbert recalled Lucian Swift's letter of three months earlier and made use of it. He wrote the *Minneapolis Journal* manager as follows: "I have noticed with interest, and, I may say, some disappointment, the comments made by the Journal for a long time past upon the new Capitol project, and especially in relation to the selection of the stone.

"While I presume the Journal will continue to do what it thinks right and proper in the matter, knowing your own interest in a certain Minnesota stone company, I would inquire whether you would wish to have me publish your letter to me of June 11th, 1897.

"For your own sake, I should very much prefer not to publish the letter, but I have felt that the attitude of the Journal has been persistently unfair and unfriendly to the Capitol project, to St. Paul, to the Commissioners and to myself. I have restrained this feeling, hoping that you would yourself in time recognize that we are trying to do the work well and thoroughly, and to build a noble and beautiful building, which will be representative of the broad intelligence and civilization of our State. . . .

"The attitude of the Journal indicates to me that you either do not understand, or do not appreciate this, and if such is to be the continued attitude of the Journal, I would like to know it, both for your sake, and my own."[15]

Swift's immediate reply was refreshingly honest: "I am very much surprised at the tone of the letter I received from you this morning. I think if you understood the situation you would not make the threat that you do. In regard to the letter I wrote you, I did it on the spur of the moment, not expecting in any way to influence your decision. . . . My interest in the company mentioned consists of a paltry five hundred dollars invested, and something that I can very well afford to lose. . . .

"As regards the Journal, I did not dictate the policy of the Journal editorially. . . . Mr. [John S.] McLain is entirely responsible for the editorial tone of the Journal, and my interests have cut no figure with him.

BRIBERY!

It Was Attempted in Connection With Capitol Stone.

Hon. John DeLaittre Approached by an Alderman.

Who Made a Direct Proposition of a $5,000 Bribe,

If He Would Vote For Kettle River Sandstone.

The most shameless attempt at bribery ever attempted in connection with a public contract in the state of Minnesota has just been unearthed by The Times. The circumstances of the crime and the character of the gentleman approached furnishes proof as strong as holy writ of the rascally methods of the "home stone" advocates, who have exhausted the whole enginery of boodle and machine politics to defeat the will of the capitol commission.

On the night before the bids were opened John DeLaittre was offered a bribe of $5,000 if he would vote for a certain kind of Minnesota stone. The kind of stone was specified. The offer was made at Mr De-Laittre's home, No. 24 Grove street, Nicollet island, and the words: "There is $5,000 in it for you if you will vote for Kettle river sandstone" were whispered in his ear by an alderman of the city of Minneapolis.

Mr. DeLaittre is too well known in this city to have his integrity questioned. He has lived in Minneapolis for thirty years and is unversally esteemed as one of her

A bribery attempt reflecting the "rascally methods of the 'home stone' advocates," uncovered by the *Minneapolis Times*, September 28, 1897

"I am sorry that the course of the Journal has displeased you, and if we have been unfair towards you or the commission, if you will present the facts in the case to me I will do what I can to have it corrected. I do not think however that you are treating me right to write the letter to me that you have. That was a personal letter to you and written only on account of our intimate relations, as I certainly would not have written to any ordinary friend. I will acknowledge that if you see fit to publish it, you will place me in rather an embarrassing situation, and it would be impossible for me to explain the circumstances and my action in regard to it. I do not wish to apologize for the letter or to hamper you in your intention in regard to it. If you think it would be fair and friendly to publish it, you certainly have that privilege, but no threat that you can make or any damage that you may endeavor to do me personally will have any effect upon the editorial columns of the Journal. I have never used the Journal to promote my personal ends, and this is the first time I have ever had it charged to me."

Fifty years earlier this exchange would have contained the ingredients for a duel between gentlemen. In the 1890s the matter came to no such dramatic conclusion. The *Journal* continued to be the one metropolitan newspaper that did not lustily cheer Gilbert and the board, but the tone of its opposition did become less vindictive and its reports of events were less strident. For example, when Governor Clough requested an opinion from Attorney General Childs on the legality of the board's decision to use non-Minnesota stone, the *Journal* for September 13, 1897, merely said that a "tremendous pressure . . . is being brought to bear upon him [the attorney general]." The fire seemed to have gone out of its rhetoric.

On September 15 Childs stated that in his opinion, while the commissioners may have been unwise, their decision was a legal one. On the same day the board signed a contract for the "General Construction of the New State Capitol Building" with the Butler-Ryan Company of St. Paul. The political stew might continue to simmer, but for the board the crisis was over. The project remained in its hands; its artistic integrity was intact. Macdonald, the spokesman for the granite regions, could only relieve his disappointment with a fine Elizabethan curse. "Our Capitol Commission . . . has cut the vitals out of one of the State's greatest industries," he said; "Damn the traitors who did the murderous deed! Let them be anathema!"[16]

The newly signed contractor began planning the next spring's work. William Baxter salvaged what he could for the St. Cloud granite industry by securing a subcontract from the Butler-Ryan Company to furnish all the granite that would go into the superstructure of the building—some $80,000 worth of stone. He assured everyone that "any granite that I take from my quarry at St. Cloud will be cut [i.e., dressed and prepared] right here." Channing Seabury turned to his private affairs which, he said, he had "neglected . . . fearfully for about three years." His fear of an ocean voyage, he told Gilbert, was the principal reason he did not accompany him across the "pond." He was referring to Mr. and Mrs. Gilbert's winter tour of architectural monuments on the continent—at their own expense, of course.[17]

The intimate correspondence between Seabury and Gilbert during the latter's overseas jaunt baldly exposes the dissension created by the board's critical sessions on the selection of stone. In February Seabury wrote with broad irony, "If you do not get back to New York until into April, our dear friend Weaver will be sadly disappointed, for he asks, with great anxiety, at every meeting, when we are going to make that trip East to meet you, and when you will be likely to be back. If it should be delayed until some time in April, I am afraid he will be busy with his spring implement business, and we shall be deprived of his society! This will disappoint you greatly, as it will myself, for I am so fond of him that I should hardly like to take so long a journey without the pleasure of his society! On this ground, therefore, solely, I must urge you to hurry back, although for any other reason that I know of, there is nothing to call you back any earlier than you may choose to come." The hot days of August 1897 had developed a split in the commission's united front. Edgar Weaver and Channing Seabury were no longer friends.[18]

Crowd at cornerstone ceremonies, July 27, 1898. White-haired territorial governor Alexander Ramsey stands near the suspended block.

4 · Laying the Cornerstone

THE WINTER OF 1897–98 was extraordinarily mild in St. Paul with the warmest January in seventy-six years; the first snow in any amount did not fall until early February. It was ideal for the capitol contractor. The Butler-Ryan firm was able to build its shops, install the machinery for stone dressing, and cart in supplies of granite and marble all winter long. As soon as temperatures stayed warm enough around the clock to allow the proper setting of mortar, the workers would be ready to proceed at full speed. But not everyone was happy. The lack of snow allowed the wind to whip dust into every crack in the city's homes, and the cutters and buffalo robes of sleighing buffs stood unused in stables and carriage houses.[1]

Walter Butler was immensely pleased with the way things were going. In mid-February, he told Seabury that he had purchased some 10,000 cubic feet of marble, which he expected to be delivered "within a few days." That material would be used to train his men in dressing marble; by the time it was prepared, the stone from his company's Georgia quarries would begin arriving regularly. Seabury was skeptical. Butler "is a pretty *smooth* individual," he wrote Gilbert, "and I do not always feel certain that everything he tells me could be proved, right up to the letter." The board's vice-president accepted few statements at face value. And he was one of the St. Paulites who complained about the lack of sleighing.[2]

By March Seabury was forced by events to change his mind about Walter Butler. "He is evidently starting in to *drive the work,* in good shape," he wrote Gilbert, "and we are all well pleased with the indications he gives of energy and push." Seabury also reported that a third of the dressed St. Cloud granite was ready and was being placed in convenient spots around the site preparatory to the masons' needs. "I think Baxter is doing good work upon it," he said. Later that year when Baxter reported to the board that he had lost $20,000 in fulfilling his contract and asked for help "on grounds of value received," the board moved "that it is the sense of this Board that it cannot allow Mr. Wm. C. Baxter any relief upon his loss as asked for in his letter." A contract was a contract, no crying over spilled milk, and the commissioners were vindicated in their feeling that Baxter had tended to underbid in the scramble for contracts on the superstructure.[3]

By July 27, 1898, it was time to lay the cornerstone with appropriate ceremony. It was a good day for such a ritual. The weather was fine. The United States was involved in what was generally considered a war of liberation against the tottering Spanish empire in both the Western Hemisphere and the Far East. Everyone was watching his newspaper for word of the occupation of Puerto Rico by American forces. (The word would come the next day.) Only the editor of the *St. Cloud Daily Times* was still upset on this fine morning. His editorial ended with the statement: "We trust that among the other documents and papers enclosed in the stone today there was placed a compilation of the anathemas poured out upon the commission by the Press and the people of the State, for their betrayal of the great State of Minnesota. Generations yet unborn should be told the story!"[4]

The parade of fifty-two units was magnificent. It was led, in a fine martial display of civilian force, by the St. Paul Mounted Police. The Fifteenth Regiment of Minnesota Volunteer Infantry was on hand, and past military glories were recalled by the ranked, if slightly stiff, members of the Grand Army of the Republic. Frontier days were represented by the presence of the Old Settlers' Association, riding in carriages. Six brass bands provided stirring music. Proudly marching and tootling among them was the *Minneapolis Journal's* Newsboys Band. Bringing up the rear, ironically enough, were St. Paul's guardians against conflagration, the fire brigade. All the members of the Board of State Capitol Commissioners and Cass Gilbert were present.

Commissioner Graves gave the introductory address. The shape of the "domed building, with impressive approaches and extensive rotunda," he told the assembled throng, conformed to public sentiment "educated with familiarity with the great capitol building at Washington." From the very beginning the will of the people had been a primary factor in the board's decisions, because the general will of society was an essential catalyst in holding together this great home of the sovereignty of the state. To make the seal even more binding Graves drew on both history and sentiment. "Upon this platform," said Graves, "there is also present the man and wife who, in 1847, took from the government of the United States as their homestead 160 acres of land of which this site and

Workers preparing for cornerstone ceremony, July 1898

a large portion of these solid city avenues form a part. I refer to Mr. and Mrs. A. L. Larpenteur of St. Paul." Auguste Louis Larpenteur, homesteader, drove the first spike when the town was surveyed.[5]

Graves was followed by the Honorable Cushman K. Davis, United States Senator, who gave the principal address. He emphasized the mission of the American nation, the moments of success in the Spanish-American War, and the commonality of the American spirit. American arms, the nation's institutions, and the great state of Minnesota could not fail, he declared. It was, said the board's report, a "powerful oration . . . the salient features of which were commented upon the day following in the columns of public print, in London, and throughout the civilized world."[6]

The climax of the ceremony came when Judge Charles E. Flandrau of St. Paul presented Alexander Ramsey with a trowel "of silver, adorned with a garland of the moccasin flower of the state; its handle is from the tamarack poles of which the old Central House, used as our first capitol in 1849, was constructed. With such a tool in the hands of such a workman, success is assured." The eighty-three-year-old Ramsey, who had been Minnesota Territory's first governor in 1849 and had later served the state in many positions, laid the mortar. A derrick lowered the stone into place, and the ritual was completed.[7]

Seabury may have felt little of the sense of providential unity that was the theme of the occasion. The board had divided over the marble issue, and it remained split into two camps. "Weaver, Du Toit, and Corliss are anxious for a 'junket,'" Seabury had reported to Gilbert at the moment of his return to New York in April, but Graves, Lamberton, and De Laittre could not go right then. "Seabury," he wrote of himself, "thinks that when the trip *is* made, he wants the 4 fellows who voted for Marble *all* to join, and he is not so particular about the others, (whose votes are generally *wrong!*)."[8]

Although the board members did not make the proposed trip, the "friendly four"—Seabury, De Laittre, Graves, and Lamberton—apparently had in mind long-range plans that might well cause additional disharmony. In his remarks at the cornerstone ceremony, Graves had publicly introduced an idea that only a year earlier he had been unable to entertain. "The interior of such a building," he told the crowd, "ought to be finished with the most beautiful of native and

Capitol construction site showing front façade of the capitol with partial walls, about 1900

foreign stone, and made an object of art, educative of the taste of our people and inspiring their pride." At last the casual contacts with the muralist society, the insistence on the use of marble for the superstructure, and the sculptured ornamentations on the sketches that were now appearing in the drawings were all brought out into the open! But, sadly, there was a fly in the ointment. Graves warned that "as it is necessary to expend practically all of the appropriation in securing a building of proper size and convenient arrangement, the commission, strictly adhering to the terms of the law . . . may be obliged to use ordinary wood work for interior finish and leave plain walls, unless the state in its wisdom shall make other provisions." A new campaign to make the interior and exterior a unified whole had begun. The acts of legislative bodies are frequently the product of pressure from the electorate, and the pressure of the electorate is often the result of strategically developed ideas.[9]

Cass Gilbert stayed somewhat in the background during the cornerstone ceremony. But in his role as architect and project superintendent he was most aggressive in his efforts to get exactly what his vision demanded. In his job of providing high-quality art and perfection in craftsmanship, Gilbert was untiring. When he began the search for a sculptor to create four figures needed over the main south entrance, he turned first to the top man in the United States — Augustus Saint Gaudens. Saint Gaudens, however, was fully engaged, his prices were too high, and he was too busy to deliver the work on Gilbert's time schedule. The architect then engaged Daniel Chester French, a popular choice whose "Minute Man" statue at Concord, Massachusetts, was familiar to every school child.[10]

The same emphasis upon quality is also discernible in Gilbert's dealings with various contractors. There is no evidence that he even bothered to reply, for example, to Walter Butler's plea that "it is impracticable to get those columns in one piece out of Georgia Marble free from flaws, seams and various other defects, as well as color." Gilbert would have sixteen perfect columns even though it exhausted the entire quarry. And he would have good workmanship. Four years later he would reject a twenty-one-foot monolithic granite column after it had been erected. A workman at the Rockville Granite Company was unlucky in roughing out the round on one of the columns, so the polishers had slightly flattened one side of it in the belief that no one would notice so small a deviation. Gilbert did notice. The imperfect column was removed from the building, and Henry Alexander's men had to carve out a perfect one. While Channing Seabury shaped his strategies and controlled his board, Gilbert would get on with his task of erecting a superbly crafted, monumental state capitol.[11]

Steelworkers placing the struts for the conical dome, about 1901. The metalwork ring takes up the outward thrust of the outer dome.

5 · The Dome

THE 1899 BUILDING SEASON of the Minnesota State Capitol project saw Cass Gilbert's spirits beginning to rise to a peak that would crest in 1902. With Seabury's able assistance, the choice of stone for the exterior had been satisfactorily compromised. The general contractor was on schedule so far, the craftsmanship was excellent, and the superstructure was shooting upward. The 1899 legislature had granted new financing with only a flicker of opposition. Gilbert's relationship with sculptor Daniel Chester French had been cordial, and the board had been persuaded to place six statues instead of four over the south entrance. The architect's spirits would continue to soar as the board maintained its string of successes in the 1901 legislature. And Gilbert would be justifiably proud when he successfully devised a unique solution to the problems of moisture and frost that had plagued dome builders since the time of Michelangelo.

The trajectory of his spirits, however, was matched by the curve of wages and prices. In the long run, the flush of success would be buried beneath the stubborn fact that the state had not provided enough money to finish the building in the monumental manner he desired. By the fall of 1902 Gilbert's spirits would sink so far that the confident architect felt defeat looking over his shoulder. In the end, it would be Seabury, the patient businessman-citizen, who picked up the cause and pushed it through to final success.

The autumn weather in 1899 was ideal for construction work. Taking full advantage of it, the Butler-Ryan crews completed all the marble work on the superstructure. The Kettle River sandstone piers for the dome were also rising through the middle of the building, and the roof trusses over the House of Representatives were nearly in place.[1] Progress since the laying of the cornerstone less than a year and a half earlier had been excellent. St. Paulites, going to and from their work, now had an exciting prospect to examine and gossip about.

Gilbert was pleased to be able to tell the commissioners that Daniel Chester French had promised that the half-size plaster models of the six symbolic figures to be placed above the main entrance would be ready for public display (and for the stone carvers) by the spring of 1900.[2] That would give people something to think about rather than sniping at the board.

French proved to be a most cooperative fellow. Even before he was awarded the contract he had sent sketches of the proposed statuary to Gilbert and solicited his criticism. "If 'Truth,'" he wrote, "is too naked for public opinion, do not hesitate to say so!" No reply exists in the architect's papers, but the finished statue (the fourth figure from the left) suggests that Gilbert felt public opinion in Minnesota was capable of accepting the nudity of a classical stone figure.[3] When a breakdown in communication resulted in the selection of blocks of marble that were too small for the planned size of the statues, French did not lose his temper. Instead he gracefully admitted that the fault might be his and gently made suggestions for righting the mistake. "The size of statuary for a building," he wrote to Gilbert," is really a question for the architect to decide ultimately. He alone can feel what is perfectly in scale and I do not feel that I can help you much, except in a matter of filling a given space. In general I think

Eight-horse team hauling block of marble up Fourth Street to the capitol, about 1899

there is more danger of getting sculpture too big and so reducing the apparent size of a building, than too small. . . . I really believe they would be large enough at the height of 65 [inches rather than the planned 96 inches]. Still, as I have said, you are the one to decide."[4]

Finally, compared to many other participants in the project, French was almost on time in completing his contract. The statuary was shipped from his New York studio on April 11, 1900. When the completed statues proved more expensive than French had estimated, it was easy for Gilbert to want to persuade the board to be somewhat generous. The relationship must have been a pleasant experience for both men. French closed out the deal by writing to Gilbert, "I think we have had a fair time together in our affair and I could only wish that all my patrons were as considerate as you."[5]

French in his New York City studio in 1921, surrounded by models including the famous Lincoln Memorial figure and, on the shelf, the male figure used on the quadriga

Gilbert was also pleased with the performance of Butler-Ryan. The general contractors had devised innovative techniques that had turned out to be efficient and cost saving. The firm had plunged into, for it, the unknown world of marble quarrying in order to reduce the profiteering of the Georgia suppliers. Knowing something of masonry (both Walter and his brother William had started as bricklayers and had been blacklisted for union activity), the Butlers had taken the then-unusual step of cutting the marble to size at the quarry, thus saving considerable sums on the freight costs. The stone was then dressed at the project site. William was especially inventive in mechanical matters. For years he had been using a steam hoist to facilitate the handling of materials on the job, and for the capitol he developed an "ingenious machine to cut varying-sized flutes in the monolithic columns" that decorated the outside of the building and surrounded the dome.[6]

The subcontractors, too, had proved superior craftsmen and conscientious managers. In spite of his financial troubles, Baxter, the granite man, had done a

Stonecutters at work on the window arches in the north façade of the building.

good job of getting out the material, dressing it, and delivering it on time. F. A. Purdy and Will J. Hutcheson, Chicago sculptors engaged by the Butlers to produce the capitals for the fifty columns in and around the building as well as other pieces of ornamentation, demonstrated efficiency and fine craftsmanship. By July 10, 1901, they had finished all the carving on the superstructure "with the exception of the hand on the little key stone figure over the main entrance arch" and were ready to go to work on the dome when needed. There they would carve the eagles that sit atop the twelve pairs of columns surrounding the drum of the dome as well as the other decorations on it. Workmanship of this sort, as Gilbert well knew, would make or break a project.[7]

Now he was ready to tackle the dome, the crowning grace of the structure. The distance between an architect's preliminary sketches and the specifications and drawings for the general contractor can be a long hard road. Gilbert's sketch for the dome of the capitol pictured a slim, graceful, and balanced ornament that gave a grave finishing touch to the whole design. How to build such a configuration presented difficult problems. Too pointed a "nose" on it might

(Above left) A Purdy & Hutcheson carver completing one of capitol's twelve stone eagles; (above) crew lowering an eagle to its permanent perch high above the city, 1901

create a skyline remindful of one of Jules Verne's rockets to the moon. A low, rounded profile would give the feeling of a county courthouse. The kind of light, graceful impact Gilbert wanted would create great difficulties in construction because the "a[e]sthetic lines" would be far removed from the "mechanical or estatic lines,"—that is, the pretty profile would not want to stand up because the thrust of its weight would be down rather than self-sustaining like the thrust of an arch. The traditional answer in the domes of St. Peter's Basilica in Rome and the Pantheon in Paris had been to construct a mechanically sound inner dome, build up its outer surface, and then bond the aesthetically desired outer dome to the inner masonry surface. The traditional solution, however, had proved undesirable because the mortar between the joints of the outer surface leaked, allowing moisture to penetrate between the finished roof and the inner dome where, because of freezing and thawing, it would break the bond between the two. The resulting damage required extensive annual repairs.[8]

Gilbert wanted to solve this seemingly unsolvable design problem. He approached it by seeking all the help he could get, consulting architects, contractors, specialists in dome building, and engineers throughout the land for months before giving the go-ahead on actual building. He investigated, from both the cost and the construction standpoints, the use of cast iron, terra cotta, and marble. In cheapness and simplicity, he found that the three materials ranked in the order listed. At this point the commissioners began to encourage him not to cheapen the structure by avoiding the use of marble for the outside finish, and finally they directed him to use that material in spite of its higher cost.[9]

The elimination of alternatives hardly simplified the problem, but it did put the board in a position to advertise for bids. On March 6, 1900, the bids were opened, and the following day the board, with only De Laittre dissenting, granted the contract to erect a marble dome to the Butler-Ryan Company for $278,734.[10] The decision must have pleased Gilbert, even though it added to the board's growing worry about the cost of the project.

The architect began again to check the construction feasibility of his design, which called for three domes. The inner one would provide a smooth decorative ceiling for the rotunda. Above that, thrusting its weight onto the corbels of the drum, would be a series of horizontally supported steel ribs angling upward to a height two inches above the outer dome; this steel cage would support the lantern providing a decorative topping for the structure. The space between the ribs of the cage would be filled with masonry to form a cone that could be thoroughly waterproofed on its outer surface, thus preventing any damage to the interior of the building by water leakage. About eighteen inches from the outer surface of the steel cone cage for the lantern, he would build a self-supporting dome of marble. The area between the cone and the marble dome would form a gutter that could drain off any water which might pass through and fall onto the cone. Thus the heaving problem created by freezes and thaws would be eliminated. Further, the self-supporting outer dome would be relatively light in weight and should, therefore, ease somewhat the problem of the thrust.

Gilbert was happy, but nervous, about the idea; the Butler-Ryan firm was sure of its ability to put up the three structures, and the R. Guastavino Company of Massachusetts and New York, which had a national reputation for dome

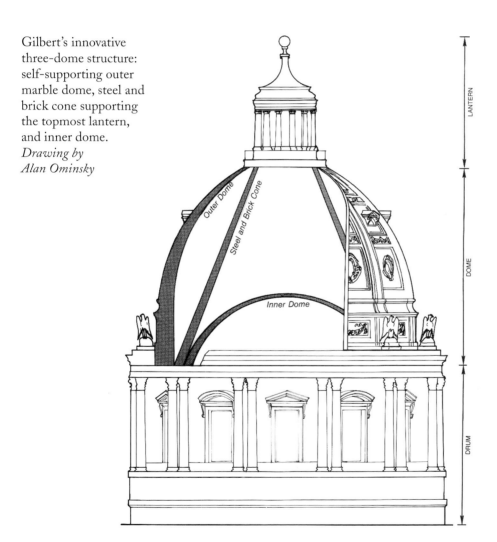

Gilbert's innovative three-dome structure: self-supporting outer marble dome, steel and brick cone supporting the topmost lantern, and inner dome.
Drawing by Alan Ominsky

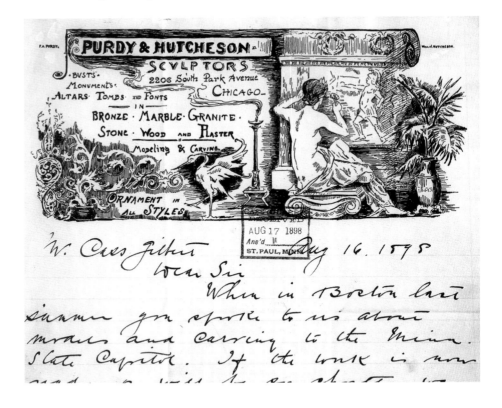

(Above) An 1898 letter
to Cass Gilbert from
Purdy & Hutcheson,
Chicago, ornamental
sculptors whose capitol
carvings included
column tops (right) with
the ladyslipper motif

building, was satisfied that the design represented a real breakthrough.[11] The steam hoist of the Butler boys began to puff away, and the massive drum began to rise above the piers that leaped upward around the edges of the rotunda. The dome was on its way.

Meanwhile, the board turned to its particular problem—money. The commissioners had at hand a report from Gilbert that contained ominous news. Although construction was proceeding rapidly and the workmanship was excellent, there was still a long way to go, and the depression, with its low wages and materials prices, was over. The board could expect prices of contracts still to be let to be 50 to 100 percent higher than had been anticipated. "This consideration," Gilbert advised, "will require even greater economy, and I shall ask your further instructions in the premises before preparing the final specifications for these contracts."[12]

Every businessman in the state was aware of the facts Gilbert presented. Members of the legislature were also cognizant of the improving economic situation. Seabury and Graves, who chaired the board's legislative committee, patiently assembled information for the lawmakers' use and appeared before the appropriate legislative committees in 1901. The compilation of facts was impressive; new capitols in Connecticut, Indiana, Iowa, Kansas, Michigan, and Rhode Island, as well as additions to the one in Massachusetts, all had cost more than the $1,500,000 available for Minnesota's building, even though all the other midwestern states had used limestone for their structures. Minnesotans, because the commissioners had patiently borne the calumny of the public for their decision to use marble, were "to have, externally, one of the most beautiful and monumental public buildings in the United States."[13]

In view of the grand effort that had already been made, the board urged that the interior be finished in a manner commensurate with the exterior. Given only the allocated funds, the job must be completed in a most inferior fashion— wooden flooring; tin roofing; plain plaster finish on ceilings and walls; only partial fireproofing; a heating plant located in the basement rather than in a separate building; plumbing, gas, and electrical fixtures that would not represent the "many improvements in this line introduced in the last few years"; and temporary steps to the east, west, and south entrances which would destroy the impressive impact of the entire building. (To those with long memories, the board's 1901 report may have recalled the seemingly innocent remarks on the finishing of the interior which Graves had made in 1898 in his speech at the cornerstone ceremony.) In short, to do the job right the board respectfully requested that the limit on expenditures be increased "by the sum of $1,000,000."[14]

One would suppose that a request for an increase of 50 percent in any appropriation for a public building would cause a tremendous furor. The Minnesota legislature of 1901 did not seem the least bit upset. Senator Hiler H. Horton of Ramsey County, chairman of the committee on public buildings, sponsored the request in Senate File 159, which sailed through the upper chamber with a minimum of comment and without a single vote in opposition on final passage. The House of Representatives duly considered and passed the increase with no real opposition and turned to the biennial budget for the five state normal schools ($273,000) and a request for $50.00 per year to be used in planting pine trees in Itasca State Park. The whole thing was almost too easy. Now the board must try to live up to its promise to have the job finished by January 1903.[15]

There was still so much to do! The normally self-assured Cass Gilbert began to push and to sound both edgy and uncertain. In June 1901 the architect received a disconcerting letter from Gunvald Aus, one of the engineers he had consulted about the design of the dome. Aus had gone over Gilbert's plans and specifications for the revolutionary design. "The general scheme," he reported to Gilbert, "is a correct and good construction." But, he continued, "I also fail entirely to see how the outer shell with the blocks cut as they now are can form a safe self-supporting dome." The marble blocks were too flimsily anchored, Aus said, and "high winds and varying temperatures would cause so much movement in the dome and between the individual blocks as to finally break off the very thin bearings of the blocks and eventually ruin the entire construction." In order to strengthen and add rigidity to the outer dome, Aus "very strongly" recommended that it be backed with a "brick shell" tapering from 16 to 8 inches. The shell, he said, could "be built up continuously with the marble" with each marble block fastened "into it with copper anchors." Then by increasing the size of the steel ring that lay at the inner base of the dome, he felt the outer dome would be safe.[16]

There is little in the records to tell us what took place during the next seventy-five days, but events suggest that neither Gilbert nor his contractor were sure what to do. Probably the architect fretted over what changes he could make in the half-completed dome to eliminate the design faults the consulting engineer had detected. When the architect is uncertain, the contractor moves cautiously and the progress of the work is bound to suffer.

In any case, by August 1901 the previously smooth relations between Gilbert and the Butler firm had been disturbed. On August 24 Walter Butler addressed the following pointed letter to Gilbert: "We have your letter of August 17th . . .

(Left) Cass Gilbert's 1897 sketch for a dome window; (above) a dome window as completed

relative to Dome . . . and note what you say therein, particularly the reference you make to us as being the cause of the delay in the work.

"Will you be good enough to point out to us in a specific and definite way wherein we are responsible for the delay in the prosecution of this work. We are not conscious of being at all to blame for this delay, and will be glad to have you inform us."[17]

Gilbert's response was equally forceful and lacking in Victorian elegance: "I think the record is sufficiently clear as to who has been the cause of the delay on this work, and it is not necessary for me to enter into a controversy with you on this question now. Should it become necessary to discuss this record in detail, my report will be made to the Board of Capitol Commissioners."

By the middle of October, Gilbert had developed a solution for the problem indicated by Aus. Before the contractor began work on the second dome, he would install a brick backing reinforced with four steel rings. This was not precisely what Aus had recommended; the job was too far along by the time his recommendation had been received, so something else had to be done. Gilbert's improvisation was apparently successful; the dome has never posed any great structural or safety problems from that time to this.[18]

Nothing more of his dispute with the Butlers appears in the record. Some accommodation must have been achieved because approximately a year later Walter Butler would send Gilbert a letter stating that the dome was very nearly finished and requesting payment for all but the clean-up work. In that interim Walter and William Butler bought out their partner, Mike P. Ryan, and changed the name of the company to Butler Brothers.[19]

August of 1901 was a trying month for Gilbert and the Butlers. While their little fracas over the dome was still in progress, another bone of contention surfaced—the tardiness of the contractor in procuring St. Cloud granite for the steps and terraces on three sides of the building. Back in April, W. C. Baxter had scribbled a little note to Gilbert which read: "For your information I wish to say that while I have lost the St. Cloud quarry on foreclosure, just about a week ago I again secured it, so that I am in position to furnish the same granite used in Basement of Capitol." He hoped that he could deal with the board directly this time rather than through the general contractor, he said, but at any rate, he was in a position to do business and would try to see Gilbert the next day. We do not know whether the meeting took place. We only know that when the contract for steps and terraces was let, Butler-Ryan received it. The contractor, replying to a "hurry up" order from the architect in August, painted a rosy picture and said the firm was doing all it could "to hasten work" on the steps and terraces.[20]

Gilbert exploded. The firm had done nothing for over thirty days, he wrote, "except possibly to negotiate inconclusively with Mr. Baxter." Such performance was unsatisfactory under the circumstances because of the time pressure and other matters. "My past experience with you compels me to say that if prompt action is not taken," he threatened, "I shall recommend to the Board that they take definite measures to enforce the rapid execution of this work, or to cancel the contract."[21]

Walter Butler's reply to Gilbert's loss of temper came from the sweeter side of the Irish. It takes two to make a contract, he reminded the angry architect. We know, he continued, that you are under pressure and that you have certain duties to perform. We would never stand in your way because we feel certain that you will not overstep your duty, "knowing as we do that you are a man of good judgement and keen discrimination, and that you will not exercise any of your delegated power or authority in a barbarous manner." Apparently the matter was not reported to the board. The contract, however, was not promptly fulfilled, because when the capitol was finally occupied in January 1905, the steps to the east and west entrances were still unfinished. They were finally completed some time before 1907 when the board made its final report.[22]

The board as well as Gilbert and the Butlers had other troubles, for the early 1900s were years of labor unrest and rising prices and wages. In the summer of 1901 a round of wage increases brought carpenters up to 35 cents an hour, stone and brick masons to 55 cents, engineers to 35 cents, and foremen to 60 cents. Although the wage increases varied for the different crafts, they had probably risen overall about 5 percent in less than a year. This fact, coupled with the rising prices of materials, made the Butlers feel that they needed prior approval on costs before accepting an emergency order.[23]

By the beginning of the next building season, the workingman all over the country was beginning to flex his muscle and to demand his share in the growing prosperity of the land. In New York City, Gilbert worried about getting the materials for the entire season from the suppliers to St. Paul before a general strike might be called "throughout the whole United States." As far as the labor situation in St. Paul was concerned, he felt it was "a very serious matter." Unless the union demands were "absolutely unreasonable" or involved "questions of principle," he recommended that the board "meet the increase demanded and pay the difference, if the contractors will not do so." Of course, he said, he "would not express this view publicly."[24]

The labor troubles, real as they were, did not result in a general national strike, although the anthracite miners of Pennsylvania did strike through a summer stained with riot and bloodshed. Construction in St. Paul was not affected, but the reaction of the capitol contractors to the labor situation and to the surging prosperity cycle caused both Gilbert and the commissioners considerable worry.

In trying to fulfill the 1901 legislature's instructions to have all jobs necessary to the completion of the project under contract by April 1902, unless the total of the bids exceeded the sum of $1,050,000, the board spent a very bad twelve months. In its *Biennial Report* of 1903, it reported that "prices of labor and materials had advanced tremendously, and also that contractors, having plenty of work to do, were not applying, in any great numbers, for contracts; and those who did bid were putting on large margins to cover their risks and insure themselves profits." Of the fifteen contracts advertised for bids between June 4, 1901, and July 1, 1902, five had to be rejected outright, three were let after modifications to reduce the cost, and only seven were accepted for work as advertised. Of the seven, three were so necessary that the board felt it had no choice but to accept the contractors' bids. Those three were for roofing and skylights, heating and ventilating equipment, and plastering. Thus the board was able to get acceptable bids on only four out of fifteen jobs.[25]

The estimates with which the board—and the legislature—were working had been made in 1896 and were based on depression prices and wages. The upturn of the economy had driven the bids upward at a frightening rate. Two of the bids the board rejected (for woodwork and painting and glazing) were 192 percent and 40 percent above the 1896 estimates. Three of the contracts granted also ran over the estimates: plastering by 74 percent, heating and ventilating by 77 percent, and roofing and skylights by 107 percent. With such cost overruns, the limitations imposed by the legislature left the commissioners helpless.

Gilbert was only too aware of the meaning of the figures facing the commissioners. In a letter addressed to Seabury's wholesale grocery house and marked "*Confidential,*" he voiced his feelings of depression. "In accordance with your request," he wrote to the vice-president, "I send you herewith an epitomized estimate of the amount necessary to complete the State Capitol in an absolutely first class manner. I have scarcely dared to add it up, for I feel very reluctant to ask any additional money for the work, and, seriously, you will recall the many times during the past year when I have urged on the Board the consideration of inexpensive interior finish. . . . I send you the figures as they work out," he wrote, "and leave it to the Board as to whether we can work on this basis or whether we must cut down the character of the work."[26]

Using updated estimates and including a quarter of a million dollars for painting and statuary as well as marble for the interior walls, Gilbert felt an additional appropriation of $1,500,000 would be required to complete the project. He provided for Seabury's use figures from comparable jobs that were under way or had been completed in the past few years. "The building has cost more than either you or I expected," he said, and much more than it would have cost had the board "been given authority to let the contracts when prices were lower. . . . I earnestly trust," he concluded, "that the Board will go forward 'with a courageous confidence in the intelligence of the community.'" The ebullience the architect had felt in 1899 was gone. In this confidential evaluation for Seabury, Gilbert now sounded tentative and almost defeatist. In spite of the board's successful relations with the legislature, the great dreams he had dreamed were dissipating under the pressure of the deadline and the upturn in the business cycle.

The problem of additional funds was now up to the board. Seabury reviewed Gilbert's estimates and suggested that they were a bit high—by about $200,000, he thought. The vice-president concluded that completion of the state's new home in a "first class manner" would require an increase of 50 percent in the spending limitation and that the final total cost of the project would be $4,500,000. Reluctant though he might be to ask for more money, Seabury accepted the problem. The board would submit a request for additional funds to the 1903 legislature.[27]

Perhaps the true temper of the man is best suggested by a charming letter that Cass Gilbert wrote to Seabury's son Paul. In it, the architect thanked Paul for sending him five photographs of their duck hunting trip during the fall of 1903: "I find them very interesting, especially the patient expression on your father's face where he stands in the blind looking in the wrong direction for ducks. I have seen him both on the duck pass and elsewhere when he did not look quite so patient."[28] We can be certain that one of the times Seabury was not "quite so patient" was during the 1903 session of the state legislature.

Cass Gilbert, a man of strong convictions who insisted on controlling all aspects of the exterior and interior design, standing atop the capitol in 1901

6 · The Legislature's Challenge

SEABURY's legislative strategy in 1903 was quite similar to that of previous years. He carefully marshalled the pertinent facts and prepared a thorough report for Governor Samuel R. Van Sant. It seems unlikely that Seabury enjoyed this task. When he accepted the position of vice-president of the Board of State Capitol Commissioners in 1893, he had never supposed that the job would drag on for a decade. But it had, and he would put forth his best effort to complete the task.

Governor Van Sant was helpful. His message to the legislators urged them to provide the additional money requested by the commissioners so they could "complete the interior to correspond with the beautiful exterior" of the new building.[1] Although the governor's statement hardly came as a surprise, it was not received with equanimity. Ralph W. Wheelock, who had begun to write a "Legislative and Political Gossip" column for the *Minneapolis Tribune,* reported on January 9, 1903, that the legislators, "so far as they have expressed themselves, believe the credit of the state is involved in furnishing the necessary sums . . . they will be disposed to insist that this appropriation be final."

With the governor on his side, Seabury sought out his respected friend, Senator Horton of Ramsey County, to sponsor the necessary bill. This powerful third-term senator, who was chairman of the committee on public buildings and a member of eight other committees, took command of the strategy and tried to hurry the legislative deliberations so that the board could get its contracts signed in time to take advantage of the summer building season. Horton's bill called for an appropriation of $1,500,000 to be financed by continuing the present mill levy assigned to the project and asked the legislature to broaden the responsibilities of the board to include providing furnishings for the building when it was completed.[2]

The board's old critic, the *Minneapolis Journal,* reported in a short item on January 14, 1903, that "several eyes opened wide when the new state capitol bill was read," and that it "caused many a frown among the country members." Editorially the *Journal* was even sympathetic: "We hope they will get it. It would be no credit to the state to botch that beautiful building by niggardly economy in the finishing touches." Editor McLain accepted skyrocketing costs as an adequate reason for the requested increase; the "builders of our new Chamber of Commerce could testify" to the correctness of the capitol commission's argument, he said. "Let the capitol be finished up in good shape," the editorial concluded, "and let the city of St. Paul get busy and clear away those old shacks in front of it which ruin the approach to the building and will spoil the effect of any ornamentation of the capitol grounds." The *Journal's* statement seemed to indicate that the last opposition had washed away in the rising tide of state pride.[3]

In a tactic planned to take advantage of the work already completed, the board invited members of the legislature to visit the new capitol and examine "an exhibit of marble and other material for interior finish . . . and other decorative

Governor Samuel R. Van Sant (1901–05), one of five governors who served during the lengthy planning, design, appropriation, and construction schedule

Newspaper jab about efforts to
win the final $1.5 million capitol
appropriation. *Minneapolis Journal*,
January 15, 1903

INSPECT THE CAPITOL

Members Visit the Building and Lunch with Commissioners.

Both houses adjourned about 11 a. m. to-day to accept the invitation of the state capitol commission to inspect the new capitol.

The commissioners were out in force with their sweetest smiles, to show the legislators how badly they needed another million and a half to complete the marble monument at the head of Wabasha street.

A toothsome luncheon had been prepared, to make the solons good-natured, and with the luncheon went a program of remarks by members and officers of the state capitol commission.

and architectural effects." It was a timeworn tactic that had usually elicited both favorable response from the legislators and much-needed press coverage of the work being done at the capitol site.[4]

This time the press coverage included the serpent in the Garden of Eden. That recently found friend, the editor of the *Journal*, commented acidly on January 15: "The commissioners were out in force with their sweetest smiles, to show the legislators how badly they needed another million and a half to complete the marble monument at the head of Wabasha street. A toothsome luncheon had been prepared, to make the solons good-natured, and with the luncheon went a program of remarks by members and officers of the state capitol commission." Neither Gilbert's earlier attempt to deal with the *Journal* nor the growing approval throughout the state had converted the paper to support the men charged with responsibility for building the capitol.

Six days later the *Journal* returned to more straightforward reporting when it covered the bill's hearing before the Senate committee on public buildings. "Mr. Seabury informed the gathering," said the *Journal* of January 21, "that no one in the state could be any more anxious to have the building completed than he. For ten years he had given the matter his attention and he was quite ready to be relieved of the responsibilities. His only request was that action be taken as soon as possible one way or the other. If the money was to be appropriated at all it should be done within thirty days for now was the time to do business with the contractors, when they were 'hungry for work' so to speak." The board must have its contracts let soon or prices in the market place would both delay the project and increase its cost. The Senate committee recommended the bill for passage.[5]

On the following day the *Journal's* editorial made a proposition that could, regardless of outcome, wreak havoc of some kind. "That fifteen hundred dollar lunch at the new capitol building the other day seems to have produced the desired effect," it began. The editorial went on to praise the idea of having "the capitol finished up in good style." Then the snake struck: "But, speaking about the capitol commission, has it ever occurred to the members of the legislature that it might be wise to audit the accounts of the commission? We do not assume that there is anything wrong or that any mistakes have been made in the expenditure of the money, but perhaps the people of the state would be just as well satisfied about that appropriation of $1,500,000 made above the original estimated expenditure if it could have the assurance of an expert investigation that the money already expended had been used to the best possible advantage." If acted upon, the suggestion for an investigation would delay the appropriation—if not defeat it—and leave the board at best with a short building season.

Senator Horton's bill came up for final vote in the Senate on January 23. His handling of the floor debate was masterful. He candidly admitted that he did not know if the board could finish its task in fifteen months with the sum being discussed, but he was certain that the board would do its duty and finish the building. Without the increased appropriation, he said, "the capitol will be finished in rough plaster like a country school house." The responsibility at this point, he implied, lay with the legislature. He quietly accepted two minor amendments which provided that $4,500,000 would be the absolute maximum for the project, including "site, erection and completion" and that "the purchase and supply of suitable and proper" furnishings for the building were to be "completed, furnished and ready for occupancy on or before the 1st day of January A.D., 1905." The bill passed unanimously.

While the Senate was deliberating, Representative Samuel A. Nelson of Lanesboro in Fillmore County was introducing in the House a resolution calling for a special committee "to audit the accounts of the State Capitol Commission." The language was nearly identical to the *Journal's* editorial of the previous day. Seabury, with admirable self-control, got off a note to Representative Ambrose Tighe of Ramsey County advising him not to oppose the resolution. The board, he said, had "sometimes wondered why we have not been called upon before." Its books were simple, clear, and in order; it welcomed the investigation. The *Journal* would have its delay, but it would not find the board trying to conceal anything.[6]

The House considered the resolution on January 26. After some maneuvering, the auditing duties were assigned to the House committee on public accounts

tach it to the seventh judicial district. Judiciary.

H. F. 82, Shearer (by request)—A bill for an act providing for an annual appropriation of $1,000 to defray the expenses of disbarment proceedings against attorneys and counselors. Appropriations.

H. F. 83, Wilson—A bill for an act to appropriate money out of the internal improvement fund to aid in building a bridge in Murray county. Roads and bridges.

H. F. 84, Putnam—A bill for an act authorizing cities to accept, acquie and hold property by gift, grant or devise, and to manage and control the same. Municipal legislation.

H. F. 85, Mark—A bill for an act relating to the expenditure of road and bridge taxes in certain villages. Roads, bridges and navigable streams.

MONEY FOR THE CAPITOL

The Appropriation of $1,500,000 for Completion Recommended by the Senate Committee.

After listening to the arguments of the members of the capitol commission for about an hour yesterday afternoon, the senate committee on public buildings concluded to recommend the passage of Senator Horton's bill increasing the limit of expense on the new capitol to $4,500,-000. This bill in effect provides an additional $1,500,000 for the capitol.

Members of the capitol commission present were Channing Seabury of St. Paul, E. E. Corliss of Fergus Falls and C. H. Graves of Duluth. The conference was a counterpart of the one held two years ago. One could almost recall the identical language of Mr. Seabury and Cass Gilbert, the architect.

It was explained that there had been an unprecedented rise in the cost of material and in labor so that the earlier estimates of the architect had been completely shattered. These were matters which the commission could not possibly foresee. Furthermore the legislature had been very tardy two years ago in voting the appropriation of $2,000,000 and the result had been to delay the work for four months because the house had held the bill for six weeks after the senate had passed it.

The members of the committee individually and collectively assured the senators that the building would surely be completed for dedication on July 4, 1904, and that the legislative chambers would be ready for the session of 1905.

All insisted that $1,500,000 would be ample to cover all expenses and that there would be no occasion for another appropriation. Mr. Seabury informed the gathering that no one in the state could be any more anxious to have the building completed than he. For ten years he had given the matter his attention and he was quite ready to be relieved of the responsibilities. His only request was that action be taken as soon as possible one way or the other. If the money was to be appropriated at all it should be done within thirty days for now was the time to do business with the contractors, when they were "hungry for work" so to speak.

The senators received the remarks of the commissioners very kindly. Senator Samuel Lord of Kasson expressed the general state sentiment when he stated that the people wanted a capitol building which would be a credit to the state and that there was no objection to voting another appropriation provided it was to be the last and that the building would be completed within a year or two. Senator A. V. Rieke announced similar views.

After the capitol commission had finished its statement and all questions had been answered, the committee went into executive session. In ten minutes the members re-appeared having voted to recommend the passage of the Horton bill.

NEW SENATE BILLS.

S. F. 47, Sunberg—Providing for the issuance of bonds by towns for building roads. Towns and counties.

S. F. 48, fl Sundberg—Authorizing the issuance of bonds by organized towns for road building. Towns and counties.

S. F. 49, Coller—Amending chapter 229, laws of 1895, relating to municipal courts in cities of less than 5,000 inhabitants. Judiciary.

S. F. 50, Dunn—Fixing representation in thirty-third legislative district (St. Paul). Judiciary.

S. F. 51, Dunn—Amending section 4,504 general statutes relating to real estate acquired by executors or administrators. Judiciary.

S. F. 52, McGill—Appropriating $2,500 for the relief of John A. Standen, hurt at state farm. Claims.

S. F. 53, Barker—Relating to the expenditure of road and bridge taxes in certain villages. Judiciary.

S. F. 54, Lord—Proposing amendment to sections 1, 2, 3 and 4, article 9 of state constitution relating to taxation. Taxes and tax laws.

S. F. 55, Lord (by request)—Legalizing certificates of sale made under mortgage powers, executions, etc. Judiciary.

S. F. 56, Brower—Providing for expenditure of tax paid by insurance companies. Judiciary.

S. F. 57, Morgan (by request)—Detaching Cottonwood county from thirteenth judicial district and attaching to seventeenth district. Judiciary.

S. F. 58, Swedback—Prohibiting counties or municipalities from incurring any liability pending proceedings to test validity of the organization of such counties or municipalities. Towns and counties.

S. F. 59, Wilson—Amending sections 1, 3, 6 and 7, chapter 154, laws of 1899, relating to probation system of juveniles. Hennepin, Ramsey and St. Louis delegation.

S. F. 6, Wilson—Amending section 1, chapter 316, laws of 1901, relating to abandonment and neglect of wife and children. Judiciary.

Urging conclusion of the contentious appropriations battles, one senator warned that the capitol would "be finished in rough plaster like a country school house." *Minneapolis Journal*, January 21, 1903

and expenditures (the initial resolution had called for a special committee that would have been dominated by outstate representatives). The eleven-man public accounts committee had only two members from the Twin Cities and one from Duluth. The others were small-town businessmen and farmers. Representative Nelson, himself a member of the committee, was apparently satisfied.[7]

Seabury was not. He sat down the next day to vent his feelings to the one man who would surely be discreet, Cass Gilbert. "There is lots of music in the air, and I do not altogether like the aspect of things," he wrote in the two-page, single-spaced letter. They were to be investigated as a result of a "squib" that appeared in the *Minneapolis Journal,* "always a friend of the New Capitol," Seabury told Gilbert ironically. The "standing committee to whom" the investigation of the commission's accounts "was referred is made up largely of farmers. . . . From the best information I have, about half of them are opposed to our bill, and there is probably not one man on the list that has had any experience to fit him to comprehend the magnitude of our transactions. . . . just now I am not enjoying life." Going to the legislature in successive sessions with requests totaling a 125 percent increase in the original appropriation was not a pleasant task. Although this was not the first time the groceryman had been depressed by the burden of his duties, it may well mark Seabury's lowest point.[8]

On January 30 he again sent Gilbert a long letter which showed a new firmness. "I want to impress on your mind," wrote Seabury bluntly, "the idea which I have that we must *husband our resources* (if this bill passes), so as to absolutely *finish* the building properly; furnish it; buy the ground at the S.E. corner of the site, and grade the entire site within the total of $4,500,000.00 for I have determined that *I* will never ask for any more. This I write you, of my own motion and unknown to anybody, with no other purpose than to let you know exactly how I feel. . . . I am ashamed . . . when I remember the promises I made to the legislature two years ago." Then he added: "My duties on this Board, during the past ten years, have probably resulted in a personal and private sacrifice of $25,000.00 at least . . . I am not willing to sacrifice my pride and self-respect in addition." Seabury had made up his mind. There would be no more excuses, no more rationalizations, no more gracious acceptances of the dictates of art; not even the uncontrollable swings of the economy would be allowed to interfere. Channing Seabury intended to complete his task. The letter's tone is not threatening, it is weary. It brooked no more discussion. The task of the moment was to satisfy the investigators.[9]

That group began its deliberations with an executive session on February 2. Its questions hinted at something more than a look into the account book.

Why, Seabury was asked, could the building not be finished without additional funds? It could be, was the answer, but not in accordance with the style and taste originally intended. "The members of the commission did not seem to be very well satisfied with the results of the first meeting," reported the *Minneapolis Tribune* of February 3, 1903. "Representative [Joseph A.] Shepard [of Minneapolis] . . . more than hinted after the meeting that while the committee had secured an expert accountant [to examine the books] . . . such examination would be the smallest part of the committee's work. 'Of course the books will check up all right,' said Mr. Shepard."

Two days later, in a move that caught everyone by surprise and raised a howl of anguish from the fourth estate, the House ordered the press and public barred from the hearings. The vote was 69 to 17. The committee began "star chamber" sessions. Little more was reported on the hearings for thirty-five days. Seabury informed Gilbert that the "expert accountant" employed by the committee was F. Wallace Hines, of whom he had never heard. By looking in the city directory, Seabury found that Hines was in the cloak, suit, and fur business. "I suppose," he said, "that the Fur business is a little dull just now, and that employment by the State on a job of this kind, at $15.00 or $20.00 per day, will be an acceptable thing to him."[10]

Governor Van Sant had a chat with the capitol commissioners and advised them to be patient. If they could, he told them, they would get what they wanted. The situation simply called for a bit of astute politicking which their friends would handle for them. The governor was probably correct, but the role he suggested was a difficult one for men of the character of the commissioners.[11]

On March 12 the House committee issued its report. The investigation had been thorough; it covered every decision and action taken by the board since its appointment; it checked every financial transaction; it examined the "proposed future expenditure recommended by the capitol commission." Not only did the committee give the board a clean bill of particulars, it commended the commissioners and their architect. In the committee's opinion, "the state has received careful and faithful services from the board of capitol commissioners." The report added "that the architect Mr. Cass Gilbert has performed his duties in every detail with the utmost fidelity, honesty, ability and skill, and that the state has received full value for the money it has expended on said capitol, and that the building promises to be an object of pride and satisfaction to the State of Minnesota."[12]

Although the issue seemed settled and the men who were building the capitol were vindicated, they had lost a valuable month. Moreover, the House had not yet considered the increased appropriation. Committees kept the bill from reaching the floor until the last day of March. Once it reached the floor, a filibuster threatened to defeat the main motion by means of a series of amendments.[13]

Representative William A. Nolan of Grand Meadow in Mower County led the charge. He wanted nothing less than dismissal of the capitol commission and its architect. Supporters of the bill received a scare when a motion to table Nolan's amendment was defeated by the close vote of 54 to 56; no one had suspected that the opponents of the bill could register such strength. Representative Tighe rose to the occasion with a grandiloquent appeal. "This capitol is not a mere ordinary building enterprise," he proclaimed, " . . . it is to be a work of art. . . . How can we compel artists to hurry when their work is to be one of the most beautiful character and to endure for all time, like the Pantheon of old, long after this form of government has passed away? . . . There will be no reward for the capitol commissioners, who have given their time and efforts for no compensation, except that a grateful state may place a tablet in that building, engraven with their names. And shall we add to that tablet that the commission was turned out of office . . . with their labor unfinished?" Then Tighe added: "This amendment is offered by the arch enemy of the bill, who is responsible for the delay upon it in this house for the past nine weeks. If you want to give him a monument, pass the amendment." The *St. Paul Dispatch* recorded that "long continued applause followed."[14]

In the cold light of time, the speech seems an overstatement, but it turned the tide. From that point on the issue was not really in doubt, although the filibuster continued. The question of the architect's fee was tossed about with considerable freedom with the facts. Friends of the bill corrected the errors. Nolan attempted a new line of attack. "There is a firm," he said, alluding to the Butlers, "that is getting most of the contracts that is making a fortune out of the construction of the building. They are very powerful and will not quit until the legislature makes them." The suggestion aroused no interest. Nolan's allusion was apparently ignored. When another opponent suggested that the new capitol was already too small and that "before long, the commission will say that we will have to have another new capitol," the *St. Paul Dispatch* of April 1 reported that "nothing but jeers greeted his remarks." The bill endured through a long rough day until at last the opposition exhausted itself and the vote was taken. It passed 103 to 5 without amendment. Governor Van Sant signed it on April 6, 1903.[15]

The delay had serious consequences. No contracts were signed until well into summer, and actual building was, therefore, limited to a short season. The board, however, had won its hardest fight. Its most consistent opposition, the *Minneapolis Journal* and the outstate legislators, presenting a populistic front to the world, had offered one final challenge and had gone down to defeat. The concept of a monument executed in the taste and style of the day had been upheld. Now the job had to be completed. Gilbert responded by examining every aspect of the task and docilely cutting costs to the bone.[16]

Cass Gilbert inspecting work on roof and dome, 1901

The capitol rotunda, 1908, with two of Edward Simmons's
Civilization of the Northwest murals on a manifest destiny theme

7 · The Interior

With $1,500,000 at hand, Cass Gilbert's despair dissipated in a flash of creativity, even though Seabury's conscience peered over his shoulder every moment. For almost eight years the architect had been playing with ideas for decorating the interior of the new capitol. The quarries of the world beckoned to him, the mural painters society found him a fine fellow to deal with, and the quadriga that he had discussed with French back in 1896 was already blazing in golden splendor in his mind. He was even able to plan seriously for a proper approach to the new building. Thanks to Seabury's skill and patience, the yeast provided by the 1903 legislature fermented a heady brew.

From the beginning Gilbert had intended to omit the classical triangular pediment above the main pavilion and to mount in its place a monumental quadriga at the base of the dome. The inspiration for the statuary was the charioteer and four horses that Daniel Chester French had modeled for the Columbian Exposition of 1893 in Chicago. French had estimated in 1896 that he could cast it in bronze for $49,500 or make it from hammered copper for $36,000. There the matter hung fire until after the final 1903 appropriation. With the board's approval, Gilbert then moved quickly. By May 19, 1903, just forty-six days after the bill became law, French signed a contract for a group containing "one chariot and human figure therein, four horses and two human figures attendant thereon . . . to be executed in copper" at a cost of $35,000. Edward C. Potter, a noted sculptor of animals, collaborated with French on the group. The technique used was that of hammering sheet copper into forms which were then riveted together over a steel frame. The whole exterior surface was then gilded by the St. Paul firm of Bazille & Partridge.[1]

The quadriga was conceived as an allegory, *The Progress of the State* (see color photos), in which mankind fearlessly proceeds toward prosperity through the concerted power of nature (the horses) and civilization (the women). The two

The monumental quadriga of gilded horses and figures in Daniel Chester French and Edward Potter's allegorical *The Progress of the State*, about 1925

draped female figures are typical of classical sculpture. A classical male figure is balanced on a chariot, holding a horn of plenty in one hand and a standard bearing the word "Minnesota" in the other. The horses are hitched four abreast with the "choke" tugs of the ancient world rather than the "collar" harness of a more modern day. The impressive gold-leaf quadriga bespeaks the conventional wisdom of its time, fitting the concept of ancient splendor that Gilbert intended to convey in his first major building.

The same intent was spelled out in the architect's handling of the building's interior. There it was curbed either implicitly or explicitly by Seabury's stern

Oval staircase (northeast of the rotunda) built on a cantilever principle rare in Gilbert's day

Rotunda and dome, about 1913, with *Civilization* mural panels by Simmons

Corridor near Governor's Reception Room with decorative ceiling paintings by Elmer Garnsey and wall sconce designed by Cass Gilbert

insistence on economy and by the recollection of the implosion of 1897 which had criticized the board's choice of Georgia marble. It would seem that neither Gilbert nor the board considered using anything except local stone for the major portions of the vast caverns of the monument. Nevertheless, Gilbert's heart went out to marble, and when Commissioner Weaver of Mankato came up with samples purportedly found near Austin in southern Minnesota, Gilbert was enthusiastic.

"On comparing it with imported marbles here," he wrote from New York to Seabury in St. Paul, "I find it in every way equal or superior to other marbles of this general type. It is so nearly the Istrian marble which was so largely used in Venice and North Italy that I can scarcely tell them apart. . . . if anything, the Minnesota marble is handsomer." If only a sufficient supply of the Austin marble existed, he said, "I think it is exactly what we want for the wall surface of our main corridors, and particularly for the rotunda." He wanted the quarry checked out immediately and, if everything looked right, leased to prevent profiteering.[2]

Gilbert felt that marble would provide a fitting background for the statuary and for the decorative bits of veined and colored stone he planned to use as accents, even though he had for several years been experimenting with both the dull buff to pinkish limestone found near Kasota in Le Sueur County and with the paler Winona limestone. He had, he told Seabury, looked into both varieties of stone, "and while I think we can use it in some places, still I do not think we can use it where it would receive any direct contact of people using the building. Both of these stones [are] absorbing, are easily marked, and not easily cleaned."[3] Gilbert's reasoning was so correct and so rational that one cannot say he was prejudiced against anything except marble, yet the temptation is great when one recalls the general eclecticism of his design and the place that marble held in the architectural lexicons of the past.

About six weeks after Gilbert had dismissed everything except Austin marble, Weaver wrote to Seabury with the facts—"there is no quarry just as I supposed." No marble existed near Austin, so it was back to Kasota or Winona limestone. The decision was made that the dull, satiny gleam of Kasota stone, when it was sliced thin and polished, would be pleasing and satisfactory and that the maintenance problem could be ignored. The acclaim accorded the capitol builders for opening new horizons for Minnesota's extractive industries was modestly accepted, and the "walls of the rotunda and corridors, piers, pilasters, arches and

Ovals of Italian marble framed in Kasota stone decorate the grand staircases' arcades, photo about 1905.

entablatures" were veneered with the warm glow of Kasota stone emanating from the very heart of the Minnesota land itself.[4]

Settling the dominant mood of the interior was only part of the strict control exercised by the one-time watercolorist who was on his way to becoming a nationally known architect. Like Frank Lloyd Wright, Gilbert viewed the architect as the dominant figure in any project. Expert knowledge of many kinds was needed, he felt, but it ought not to be divided up among a committee of experts. "We live in an age," he once said, "that has the fad to credit man with 'specialties,' and a 'specialist' seems to be considered in every walk of life. In art there should be no 'specialists,' or at least the lines of subdivision should be very slight. In the old days the architect, painter and sculptor were frequently one and the same man. There is no reason why this should not be so now."[5]

As the twentieth century dawned, the orthodox world of architecture and architectural decoration in America was operating at the far end of a decided cultural lag. As late as 1913 Edwin H. Blashfield, one of the country's early

Rotunda column with molded plaster ladyslipper-motif capital

mural painters, would write that "the sculptor and painter must believe in the architect as commander-in-chief, leader, designer, and creator of a whole, which they are to enhance *as* a whole by their art; and again they must see in him the planner of interrelated parts whose interrelations they must help, not hinder." The acceptance of leadership by the architect would not diminish the artist's contribution; indeed it guaranteed that "beauty will come after it as surely as harvest after seed-time."[6]

Mural painters at the end of the nineteenth century believed that the purpose of their art was an abstraction called harmony and beauty, blending into the space assigned them by the architect. They not only accepted his decision on matters of shape, amount of space, subject matter, and the colors to be employed, but also solicited his criticism while their compositions were in the planning stages. The negation of freedom of expression and execution in mural painting implied in this attitude was made quite clear in the opening lines of the preamble of the constitution of the National Society of Mural Painters, which stated that the aim of the society should "be to promote the delineation of the human figure in its relation to architecture . . . and at the same time to foster the development of its ornamental concomitants."[7] There was no stand for treating the humanness of the human figure or for seeking to express the human condition in either a world of joy or sorrow; there was only a commitment to help the architect ornament his spaces. In short, the mural painters were urged to foster what might be considered a condition of anemia in their art, to reduce the full-bodied, full-blooded, full-passioned figures of their Renaissance predecessors to thin, two-dimensional decorative figures.

Although harmony between architect and painter was a mutual goal, both were very aware of the third party ultimately responsible—the commissioners. In 1904 the conscientious Board of State Capitol Commissioners handed its architect a little surprise. Its members were coming east on an official visit, Seabury announced to Gilbert, to see what the artists were doing. "To have all these important things being prepared down there," he wrote, "without our having any knowledge of them, other than photographs and small sketches, does not quite suit some of us. . . . Ignorant as we all are, in the realm of art, we yet feel that we have brains enough to know what we like, and to form some opinion as to what the great mass of our people will like, hence it is not impossible that some one of us might have an idea, or possibly could throw out a suggestion, that would not utterly ruin or dishearten the gentlemen who are working on these things, but, on the contrary, might be useful to them." Such visits were guaranteed to pose the greatest possible threat to the professional

The capitol's Kasota stone rotunda with decorative north stars and Edward E. Simmons's *Civilization of the Northwest* mural panels

The west wing
staircase leading to
the Senate Chamber
(opposite) and
Henry O. Walker's
lunette mural,
*Yesterday, Today, and
Tomorrow* (above)

House of
Representatives
Chamber and
decorative ceiling
painting

The Governor's Reception Room with elaborate gold-leafed woodwork, crystal chandelier, and commissioned paintings by Francis D. Millet and Howard Pyle

The Battle of Nashville, by Howard Pyle, hanging in the Governor's Reception Room

Supreme Courtroom with mural by John La Farge

Rathkeller restaurant (opposite), and restored German motto: "May God bless your entrance and exit" (above)

Cigar box label published about 1905 in St. Paul

Gilded quadriga sculpture by Daniel Chester French titled *The Progress of the State*

The capitol mall looking toward the Mississippi River, with downtown St. Paul
on the left and the cathedral on the right

standing of the artists and to their artistic integrity. Apparently, however, the group of Minnesota businessmen proved amenable and did not prick the balloon of harmony.[8]

Gilbert did everything he could to allay any fears of interference the artists might have had by including a clause in each man's contract that made him a member of an advisory "Board of Design." Thus each was reassured that questions concerning his composition or color scheme would be answered by fellow professionals and not by a lay group uninformed about painting or sculpture. Apparently the advisory board never met formally, and its members were only twice asked for their judgment on some preliminary sketches submitted by the artists. Gilbert's active supervision through correspondence and visits kept the widely scattered group working as a team.[9]

Garnsey's stenciled and hand painted ceiling decorates the Rathskeller, based on the German tradition of a city hall (*ratshaus*) restaurant in the basement (*keller*), about 1913

Thus the capitol's interior was, in the spirit of the times, Cass Gilbert's creation. The tone of the whole was firmly established by his selection and use of materials. He designed the enormous *Etoile du Nord* that dominates the translucent glass circle in the floor of the main rotunda, tipping the points of the eight-pointed star with red Numidian (African) marble and providing a good measure of natural light for the large circular basement room directly underneath. He carried the circular form upward to the dome by accenting three levels with circles. He surrounded the main floor rotunda with a circle of arches supported by piers veneered with Kasota stone; the open area of the rotunda on the second floor was girded by balusters of Hauteville (French) and Skyros (Greek) marble; and the third circular accent was provided in the form of ornamental ironwork in the dome itself high above the third floor (an area not open to the public). The motif was finally capped by hanging a large crystal chandelier in the center of the rotunda area just below the dome's ceiling.[10]

The grand staircases to the right and left of the main rotunda (see color photos) that lead to the second floor were made of Hauteville marble because it strongly resembled the soft warm tone of Kasota stone but was harder and could take more wear. The balusters of the stairwells were Skyros marble and the spandrels between the arches on each side of the stairs were of imported Breche Violette and Old Convent Sienna. The ovals of Italian marble were framed in Kasota stone. Gilbert selected the variegated-colored *Breche Violette* marble for the thirty-six columns that surround the two stairwells on the second floor. In the second floor rotunda area, a few feet from the balustrade, the circular form becomes octagonal. The walls were veneered with Kasota stone and display the forms of the piers that thrust upward to support the dome. In each of these piers was a niche intended for statuary, an inlaid panel of Old Convent Sienna marble from Italy above, a seat of Skyros marble below, and double pilasters on either side. Just above the niches, Gilbert designed a wide inlaid band of the red stone—long revered by Native Americans—from the Pipestone quarries in southwestern Minnesota. In the four open spaces between the piers, he placed great columns of Minnesota granite: the north and south columns are deep bronze in color from the Ortonville quarries, and the east and west monoliths are purplish gray from Rockville.[11]

For the Senate chamber in the west pavilion, he chose Fleur de Peche (French) marble for decorative accents. He used white Vermont marble for the House chamber in the north pavilion and red Numidian marble on the fireplaces in the retiring rooms of both House and Senate. He repeated the austere white Vermont marble for the Supreme Court in the east pavilion. All three chambers in the extending pavilions have unobtrusive skylights that allow the soft flow of natural light to fill all corners of the rooms. Gilbert also placed skylights over the grand staircases. Even the rotunda receives a share of natural illumination from the twelve windows that pierce the dome.

In what, for him, was typical attention to detail, he designed an exciting oval staircase of Joliet limestone just off the northeast side of the rotunda. An uncommon design at the turn of the twentieth century, the cantilevered stairs were fastened on one end only to a rigid vertical support inside the wall. Thus each stair literally hangs from the wall, providing a fine sense of unobstructed upward motion in what is normally a very static functional element of design. It was Gilbert who created the gopher as a decorative motif for the iron grillwork that guards the main floor stairwell to the basement and the showy ladyslipper (Minnesota's state flower) that dominates the carvings on the capitals crowning each interior column.

In short, if the mural painters of the turn of the century wanted to work on a team where the architect was a commander in chief who would lead them aggressively, Cass Gilbert was their man. He set the goal firmly in his design, his selection of materials, and his color tones. Like his mentors, McKim, Mead and White, he felt compelled to select his modes from the past. Like them, too, he made the design his own and imposed the genteel tastes of his era. He would be monumental but he would not be triumphant; his color tones would be warm but they would not spring out with exciting reds and yellows. He would create solidly and substantially, using modern engineering techniques, but he would subdue his creation under the suavity of a Victorian gentleman on public display.

Kenyon Cox, who painted some of the mural decorations for the project, caught the point in an article he wrote for the *Architectural Record* in 1905. The architect for the Minnesota State Capitol, said Cox, "has desired an effect of sumptuousness and subdued splendor, and has become a colorist as well as a draughtsman. His distinction is that he has never allowed richness to degenerate into gaudiness or beauty of material to disguise beauty of design. If he has handled color like a painter, he has done so like one of the old painters, whose work, though it may lose much by translation into black and white, yet retains its essential quality in a wood-cut."[12]

Cass Gilbert's Minnesota capitol would be a monument to that moment in history when the good Queen Victoria of England set the manners, the morals, and the aesthetic taste of the Anglo-American world with her utilitarian mood, her quietistic tastes, and her genteel habits. In leaving behind the raucous features of the frontier, Minnesota would go all the way back to the mother country.

Governor's Reception Room, elaborately decorated with large oil paintings commissioned for its walls, 1913

8 · The Painters

FOR THE CAPITOL'S PAINTERS, the project became a reality early in 1903 after the legislature granted the Board of Commissioners a 50 percent increase in the limit on its expenditures. The commissioners' role in decorating the interior was quickly done when they helped Gilbert decide on the subject matter. In characteristic nineteenth-century American fashion, they selected "subjects that would appropriately represent the growth and progress of the Northwest in the direction of manufactures, commerce and agriculture from pioneer days to the present time." The West would one day become an imaginative symbol for the American people, but while it remained only a geographical entity, its settlers were interested in displaying their efforts to become as civilized as the East from whence many of them had migrated. Channing Seabury was proud of the achievements of his adopted state, but it was a pride tinged with something of an inferiority complex. To the representative citizen of turn-of-the-century Minnesota, the meaningful subject to be depicted in its history was its progress from wilderness to civilization, from prairie and forest to city. In this topic could be revealed the whole of life's effort and the citizen's pride. But it should not be treated in too straightforward a manner. The commissioners felt that the subject "would probably have to be treated allegorically," perhaps fearing that the vigor and strength of the paintings might overwhelm the architecture rather than ornament it. Nevertheless, in creating the allegories, they told the artists, "care must be taken not to fill the building with Greek gods and goddesses, as these were considered inappropriate for a building devoted to the transaction of business."[1]

After the commissioners had developed their extensive directive outlining what they wanted, Gilbert acted in his usual fashion. He contacted the four most famous names in mural painting in the country; he seemed to make no effort to find local artists. For the big job of decorating the interior, he signed

Elmer E. Garnsey, who had been in charge of the team of mural painters that had decorated the Library of Congress in Washington, D.C., six years earlier; Edwin H. Blashfield, who had created the murals in the dome of that library; Edward Simmons, who had made a major contribution to the mural work at the Columbian Exposition of 1893 in Chicago; and John La Farge, the dean of American muralists. Later Garnsey would employ two well-known men, Kenyon Cox and H. O. Walker, as associates; they would execute the murals for the skylight walls of the grand staircases and the lunettes over the Senate and Supreme Court chambers (see color photos).[2]

The group of mural painters worked as individuals in St. Paul, New York, Paris, and other places. Under Gilbert's direction, in the short space of four years, they would transform the rest of the interior—the rotunda dome, the corridors, and all the public rooms—with a pastiche of colors and figures that allegorically spelled out Minnesotans' view of their place in the sun. Garnsey would do much of his work in St. Paul. He would cover the lunettes above the windows in the dome with signs of the zodiac and the corridor ceilings and those of the House of Representatives with elaborate stylized designs that gave color and life to otherwise ordinary plaster. His bold flat designs in crimson and gold for the Senate retiring room (not open to the public) would stand as vibrant reminders of the responsibilities and traditions of the office. He also took charge of the lesser work that was so important to the unity of the whole decorative scheme.[3]

Of the major murals, Simmons' allegory *Civilization of the Northwest* in the rotunda (see p. 74 and color photos) may be taken as typical of the subject matter and the compositional methods employed in the capitol. In the first of its four panels a youth, whose proportions are strongly classical, leaves home (the East) in the company of Hope and the Greek goddess of wisdom. In the second panel the young man rids the West of its noncivilizing features—the bear (representing savagery), the cougar (cowardice), a woman bearing a deadly nightshade plant (sin), and a man bearing a sprig of stramonium (stupidity). In the third panel mature man rips stones from the soil and releases wealth and fertility. Finally, resting from his labors, the man sits clothed in the cloak of Wisdom and directs the four winds to carry out his will. The little tale is flattering to the pioneer and is a clear-cut, understandable expression of the then commonly accepted social theory of God-given progress toward a divinely conceived destiny for America. The uncertainties implied by the work of scientists like Albert Einstein, by international disruptions like the world wars, or by the economic collapse of

the depression of the 1930s had not yet struck. For a moment Americans could look upon their land only with pride. Today Simmons' allegory may seem a bit smug and self-satisfied, but in his day it merely expressed Minnesotans' attitudes.

Except for La Farge's murals in the Supreme Court chamber and Garnsey's decorations in the House of Representatives retiring room (not open to the public), the subject and treatment of the other mural paintings in the capitol reflect similar social attitudes. In the Senate, Blashfield's two lunettes depict *Discoverers and Civilizers Led to the Source of the Mississippi* (see p. ii) and *Minnesota the Granary of the World*. The former treats the American Indian in the tradition of the eighteenth-century concept of the Noble Savage and is typical of the treatment of the Indian in all the capitol paintings. The granary scene is interesting because of its portraits. The central female figure is modeled after a popular actress of the day, Mary Anderson. On the left side are portraits of Channing Seabury and Cass Gilbert.[4]

Garnsey's effort in the House retiring room differs from the others in realistically rather than allegorically depicting the flora of the state in a pleasing and quiet composition. Edith Seabury Nye, who as a child knew most of the capitol artists as guests in her father's house, recorded the contribution of an anonymous Irishman to this mural. While he was filling in the colors for Garnsey, the Irishman "put in a shamrock and Mr. Garnsey remonstrated with him saying, 'But, Pat, shamrocks don't grow in Minnesota,' and his answer was 'shure an' if they don't yet, they will' and Mr. Garnsey admitted with a grin that he let him leave it."[5] The shamrock remains to this day just to the left of the fireplace mantel.

The Supreme Courtroom (see color photos) holds the best examples of traditional mural art in the Minnesota State Capitol—four lunettes painted by John La Farge. Like the others, they are allegorical, but La Farge selected four moments in history to illustrate four significant advances toward the modern concept of the relationship of law and society. The first lunette, *The Moral and Divine Law*, depicts Moses on Mount Sinai and represents human conscience and divine law standing between civilization and savagery; the second lunette, titled *The Relation of the Individual to the State*, illustrates Socrates at the home of Cephalus, where he is expostulating on his idea that the "true artist in proceeding according to his art does not do the best way for himself, nor consult his own interest, but that of his subject." The third mural, *The Recording of Precedents*, shows Confucius collating and transcribing documents to emphasize the importance of the past and of precedent. (Edith Nye said that "after

The Moral and Divine Law, one of four murals by John La Farge in the Supreme Courtroom

the painting was entirely completed" and La Farge had "painted Confucius in a yellow robe, some book he was reading mentioned that the great Chinese philosopher hated yellow, so La Farge repainted his robes and almost the whole picture.")[6] The fourth lunette, titled *The Adjustment of Conflicting Interests*, reflects on the importance of equity as Count Raymond of Toulouse seeks to balance the interests of the citizen, the church, and the state. While La Farge's compositions fill a prescribed space and seek no integrity of their own, the modeling and coloring are strong and free. Within the context of the nineteenth-century tradition of mural painting in America, they represent something of the best.

La Farge's dealings with the board were marked by difficulties. All contracts dealing with the new capitol were paid piecemeal; after a certain portion of work was completed, reported by letter to the board, and certified by Gilbert as the superintendent of construction, a check equaling the percentage of the total job represented by the completed work was issued by the state. La Farge signed a contract for $40,000 to do "four large lunettes" on September 28, 1903. Ten months later he requested an additional $2,500 for work that Gilbert had certified as completed. On July 6, 1904, the board refused the request on the grounds that so far La Farge had done nothing except direct his assistants in designing the paintings and sketching the designs on canvas with charcoal crayon. Seabury wrote La Farge that the board could not in good conscience advance any more public money until it had seen "the work of your own hand" in some part of the pictures completed with "permanent painting in oils." [7]

La Farge hit the roof. In a seven-page reply he condescendingly blamed the misunderstanding on Seabury and delivered a veiled threat not to finish the contract. "You may not be to blame," he continued, "for not understanding matters outside of your habit and knowledge, but in such matters and in all conduct with business, it is dangerous and unadvisable to go outside of one's experience, and against the opinions of experts. All experts of understanding could understand the correctness of what I intend to explain to you. . . . I shall not take up your letter in detail at present. My method of answering you may make you understand how irrelevant many of your observations are." [8]

Then followed five close-typed pages of pedantic introduction to the art of mural painting, concluding with a grand pronouncement on La Farge's own skill and another try at defending his honor without personally insulting

Francis D. Millet's 6 x 10-foot oil painting, *The Treaty of Traverse des Sioux*, hangs over the fireplace in the Govenor's Reception Room.

the vice-president: "I repeat that it would be an injustice to you, that is to say the work that you represent, that anything should be done against the habits of the profession and especially against mine, since I am alone responsible for it. If you were it would be another question. But if you allow this to be carried out in the proper practical and professional way, you may point with pride to the fact that you chose me to give adornment and beauty to the walls of the building in your charge."

Seabury's reply gave as good as he got. "I am sorry," he began, 'that you did not reply to my letter of the 8th more specifically. . . . The views held by our Board are very fully outlined . . . [therein]; and I find nothing in yours . . . to change them. We have paid you now the quite handsome amount of $13,500, and surely that ought to have been sufficient to cover all the various expenses. . . . I do not think you are justified in the position you take, and I think you should drop all this contentious spirit, and go ahead with your individual work on at least one of the pictures. . . . There is nothing particularly new in the lengthy explanations you give," he wrote. "Of course, no artist like yourself would jeopardize his personal standing and reputation by negligent, careless or superficial preparations for the work he had undertaken, and as you rightly say, both yourself and ourselves would be criticised, were you to do so. We have had no fear of this whatever, in your case. . . . Further correspondence is unnecessary."[9]

La Farge's anguished 294-word answer sped to St. Paul via telegraph on August 8, 1904. Seabury calmly replied: "Our Board duly considered all the questions raised by you, and passed a voucher in your favor for the sum of $2,500.00 The same

Decorative artists and designers who work is seen in the capitol, 1904

was committed to my care with instructions . . . to deliver it to you, whenever I shall have been advised by our architect, Mr. Gilbert, that he has personally seen one or more of your pictures showing satisfactory progress towards completion in the direction of final painting in oils."[10]

Seabury then settled back to wait. Do not contact La Farge, he advised Gilbert; "let him notify you when he wants to *show you* some *painting in oil.*" Two months passed. On October 12 Seabury received a handwritten note from F. W. Mitchem, attorney for La Farge. Mitchem was in the city on another legal matter, the note said, and would like to have a chat with Seabury and Gilbert about his client's "relations with your capitol commission." We can only assume that the conversation resulted in some agreement, since no record of it has been found. We do know that a letter from Gilbert, dated November 14, was read into the minutes of the board. He had been informed that the Moses painting was on exhibit, he said. "I made a formal but brief 'inspection' of the picture, and I therefore notify you that I understand that the terms of the resolution of the Board have been formally complied with and the payment for the fourth cartoon should be made. I enclose a certificate for the same." Seabury then reported to the group that the previously drawn check had been forwarded to the painter.[11]

La Farge may have had the last word on the subject. When he was painting his picture of Confucius (the last of the four canvases to be executed), Royal Cortissoz, his friend and biographer, wrote that La Farge had pictured the Chinese sage reading from a scroll on which "La Farge got Okakura [an assistant] to help him inscribe in Chinese characters one of the Sage's sayings, 'First the white, and then the color on top.'" Cortissoz believed that this was a "playful comment" on a disagreement between La Farge and his fellow muralists as to when an artist should begin color studies for a mural—before or after the completion of the black-and-white cartoon for the composition. It seems possible that the comment may have been directed at Channing Seabury and the Minnesota Board of State Capitol Commissioners for holding back a paycheck.[12]

For the governor's reception room—probably the most elaborately decorated in the building—the board commissioned six paintings by four nationally known artists. The heavily wainscoted room (see color photos), with its plaster casts of regional fruits and seeds gilded with gold leaf, its heavy, stained white oak woodwork, and its fireplace of Fleur de Peche and Levanto marble, was "sumptuous in its every appointment."[13] Here, the commissioners directed, were to be hung six paintings illustrating glorious moments in the history of the state. Francis D. Millet was chosen to do a Civil War scene and one showing the signing in 1851 of the Treaty of Traverse des Sioux, which opened most of southern Minnesota to white settlement. Douglas Volk also did a battle painting and one showing Father Louis Hennepin at the Falls of St. Anthony in 1680. Rufus F. Zogbaum painted the famous Civil War battle of Gettysburg, and Howard Pyle depicted the battle of Nashville.

Five of the six—the four Civil War scenes and the treaty painting—are of interest to historians. They are filled with portraits of the leaders of events considered notable in the memories of people in 1903, and thus regarded as fitting subjects for the state capitol. Some of the living heroes themselves or their photographs were available to the artists of the battle pictures. Some of the people present at the treaty signing were also available to Millet for portrait purposes, and a young painter, Frank Blackwell Mayer, had attended the treaty ceremonies in 1851 and recorded the scene on canvas. Mayer's painting provided good source material for Millet's re-creation. Volk was not so fortunate. For his depiction of Father Hennepin at the Falls of St. Anthony, he had to rely upon written sources. Volk, Gilbert, and Seabury spent a great deal of time researching the subject and developing the scene with as much historical accuracy as possible.[14]

Howard Pyle, a Quaker who was disappointed when he did not receive the commission to do the battle of Missionary Ridge, overcame his chagrin and created the most widely known painting of the six, *The Battle of Nashville* (see color photos). Pyle made his greatest contribution to the world of art by illustrating periodicals and children's books. Perhaps it was his skill in the use of line that enabled him to catch the intensity and excitement of the crucial moment of a bayonet charge. The success of the composition lies in the emotion created by the use of dynamic line and restless mass rather than in representing the individual men. The whole is remindful of the works of two French romanticists, Théodore Gericault and Eugène Delacroix, whose efforts did so much to open the door for the development of abstractionism in modern art.[15]

The board expended a total of $231,500 for mural and framed paintings in the capitol, and both the commissioners and the art critics of the day were more than satisfied.[16] The collection is important for our time because it contains examples of the beginning of modern mural painting in America. In its entirety the art reflects a unique moment in the history of public art. In this single, magnificent building one witnesses the transition from an allegorical painting style expressing lofty virtues to one reflecting the young state's desire to document its contribution to the history and development of the United States. The result is a unique expression of high-minded civic ideals and popular taste that deserves to be protected and displayed.

Veterans carrying tattered battle flags out of the old capitol on June 14, 1905

9 · The Capitol Completed

WHILE FINISHING, decorating, and furnishing the interior of the capitol was the major task remaining to be done in April 1903, various exterior details also had to be completed. The granite terraces and steps were not in place (a strike of granite workers had slowed down that contract); the equipment in the power-house for direct current lighting as well as the heating and ventilating systems were unfinished. Then there was the matter of securing through condemnation proceedings three acres on the southeastern portion of the site in order to improve the symmetry of the grounds. Building the roadways and sidewalks, grading the entire area, covering it with black earth, seeding it with grass, and landscaping it would be done later. When the legislature occupied the new capitol for the first time in January 1905, the board reported that $162,150 of its appropriation remained to take care of such details as were not already under contract.[1]

By the time the entire job was finished in 1907, the board was able to report that the total cost was $4,458,628.27. The sum of $41,371.73 remained unexpended, a fact which must have pleased Channing Seabury very much. Of the funds spent, $108,672.32 had gone for furniture, $25,805.64 for carpets and draperies, and $388.97 for postage and stationery. The latter covered a period of thirteen years and eight months. During that same time, the board had expended $23,512.02 for the per diem and traveling expenses of the seven commissioners, or about $245 apiece per year. The architect's fees for plans, specifications, and superintendence of construction totaled $173,862.16, or roughly $15,800 per year for the eleven years that he was engaged. It would seem that the small group of businessmen who composed the board had succeeded in giving the citizens of the state their money's worth.[2]

All the bills, however, were not paid in 1907. The board had outstanding certificates of indebtedness amounting to $2,850,000. Except for $10,000, the

Gilbert's sketch
for a capitol
hallway bench

entire sum was held by the Investment Board for the Permanent School and University Funds of the state, where it drew 3 to 3½ percent interest. All of the certificates would be paid off by July 1, 1935.[3]

One other cost of the building was recorded in the architect's monthly report to the board dated July 9, 1903. On June 25, 1903, he reported that "a laborer employed by the Butler Brothers, in removing rubbish fell from the scaffolding at the intersection of the north corridor of the east stairway of the 2nd story Rotunda corridor. He fell to the basement floor, a distance of about 32 ft., and was almost instantly killed. This I believe is the 6th man killed in the course of the construction of the Capitol building." It was the last death noted in the records.[4]

The inevitable problem of cleaning up the exterior marble work also engaged the board's attention and study. In view of the damage that had been done to New York's city hall by sandblasting the marble, the board could not recommend that method. In the end, the capitol contractor used soap, water, sponges, and pumice stone, a method "which accomplished good results, as will be seen by examination," said the board's 1905 report.[5]

Such a bland summary of the period from 1903 to 1907 scarcely conveys a sense of the inevitable crises that always accompany the final finishing and occupying of a new building. For example, there was the matter of space for the newspapermen. Seabury's friend, Senator Horton, urged him to "*not* make any provisions for news-paper reporters on the floor of either the Senate or the

House." "He tells me," Seabury wrote, "that notwithstanding the fact that no member of either house would like to assume the responsibility of making this radical change from past custom, nevertheless they will unanimously welcome the removal of all news-paper men from access to them on the floor of either House, and thank us for assuming the responsibility. . . . Nothing that we could do would so much relieve and please them, as to provide for comfortable and satisfactory quarters in some portion of the galleries *on the next floor.*" To accommodate the senator's wishes, the Flour City Ornamental Iron Works of Minneapolis installed two brass railings to delineate the reporters' space in the House and Senate galleries.[6]

The reporters had something to say about the matter, however, and the legislators, who were not responsible for the arrangement, were quick to respond. The first session in the new building began on January 4, 1905. The next day both

Flags fly on the finished capitol awaiting installation of the quadriga, 1905

the House and Senate reacted against the arrangement. Representative Joseph T. Mannix of Hennepin County remarked that "the present accommodations [in the gallery] are wholly inadequate. . . . Although the rules committee may not grant concessions now it is only a question of time until the newspaper men will be brought down onto the floor." In the upper chamber Senator George P. Wilson of Hennepin County offered a resolution instructing the custodian or the sergeant at arms "to provide a suitable table or tables on the floor of the senate for the use of said reporters." Only a few days elapsed before the reporters were returned to the floors of both chambers. So responsive were the legislators that they did not find it necessary to consult either the Board of State Capitol Commissioners or the architect.[7]

Then there was the matter of wastebaskets. Seabury had written to Gilbert about them in 1904, commenting that "there is a great variety of these articles and some of them are far from ornamental, so that I think *we* should select them." A week later he was back again on the topic of such accessories as wastebaskets, inkstands, match safes, and similar items. "I want to have those legislative halls and committee rooms so satisfactorily furnished," he said, "that we may have an immediately responsive chorus from the members of the two Houses when they convene." The vice-president's voice was heard, and appropriate accessories were provided.[8]

Meanwhile the architect was worrying about everything from doorknobs (those he designed were too heavy and broke off easily), to toilet fixtures, to the kinds of trees used for landscaping. Gilbert wanted poplars, junipers, trimmed evergreens, and bay trees in tubs properly placed to show off the entrance. The miscellaneous correspondence, especially for 1903–05, sounds a bit like the private conversations of a young couple furnishing their first home; as one stops to consider, the analogy may be appropriate. In spite of all the minor crises, the governor's quarters were sufficiently prepared so that Governor Van Sant could occupy them late in 1904, a little before the end of his term.[9]

If Seabury and the commission were beginning to feel possessive of their charge, Cass Gilbert felt positively paternalistic toward his brain child. In a 1904 memorandum, he laid out a plan for the city of St. Paul that would ensure the best possible vistas for his monumental creation. He proposed that "the immediate surroundings of the building" be enlarged and made symmetrical, that properties east and south of the capitol be purchased and developed as public gardens in order to prevent the erection of tall buildings between the capitol and the downtown St. Paul business district, that the capitol site be extended all the way to Archbishop Ireland's new cathedral at Summit Avenue, and that "a broad avenue" be constructed "to the south of the center axis of the main front of the building, crossing the city to Seven Corners." He also suggested that the open areas in this plan be used as parks and gardens decorated with statuary and flights of stairs.[10]

Gilbert's proposal was reminiscent of the sixteenth-century philosophy of baroque city planners which required "the subordination of the contents of urban life to the outward form." It was a grandiose design, remarkable for an architect of that day and for a turn-of-the-century city in the midwestern United States. It was perhaps too grandiose, but the broad outlines of Gilbert's plan have been partially implemented.[11]

While Gilbert was dreaming of the future, the wheels of politics in public architecture were grinding away in the 1905 present. The building on which the commissioners had lavished so much care and attention for twelve years was about to pass into the hands of elected officials where it would be subjected to

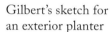
Gilbert's sketch for
an exterior planter

the kind of treatment that patronage and short tenure provided. In an effort to counteract that event, the board offered a proposal: "The State of Minnesota is about to occupy her new home—a palace, in comparison with any of its kind heretofore constructed in the West. . . . We do not believe that it can be properly cared for and preserved, if left to frequently changing and inexperienced hands. We find upon inquiry that the prominent large modern buildings of a similar type elsewhere are placed in the exclusive charge of non-political boards or individuals with complete authority, and so, we think, ours should be."[12]

A bill designed to establish a precedent for a permanent capitol commission was successfully pushed through the upper house by Senator Horton, giving the board control of the building for another two years and empowering it to purchase all fuel and supplies and hire all employees needed to care for the capitol. The bill also provided that one member of the board would be selected as a "resident supervisor" at a salary of $3,000 per year. (The assumption was that the person selected would be Seabury.) When Senator Lars O. Thorpe of Kandiyohi County objected to the unseemly haste, Horton replied that the legislation was needed "to provide immediately for the care of the building. It is an emergency measure. . . . The janitors, firemen, engineers, scrub women, and other employes who are now at work in the building are practically working on trust; there is no method for paying for any such services." Horton assured the Senate that the bill was not a scheme to steal patronage from the governor; after the building was completed, "the commission can relinquish all control." What the senator did not say was that no Democrat had been re-elected as governor in the history of Minnesota; in two years he anticipated a friendly Republican in the governor's chair.[13]

Replying to an inquiry from a Wisconsin citizen, Seabury was more forthright. The hullabaloo over the new building, he said, was simply a political battle with the newly elected Democratic governor, John A. Johnson, over patronage. "Our Board has been advocating *a permanent Commission* to care for the beautiful structure," he wrote, "rather than to let it drift into the hands of political appointees, and be changed every two years, with each change of administration. Unfortunately, we have, at this time, a Democratic Governor, elected in a State which gave every other Republican candidate a majority . . . and this whole fuss that is being made is for the purpose of defeating our efforts for a permanent Commission to care for the building, and to save *the patronage . . .* to the new Democratic Governor."[14]

The Horton bill had a somewhat different fate in the House. By the time its opponents finished offering amendments, the sinecure of the resident supervisor had been eliminated. The board was left in control until the building was completed, and it was empowered to employ a custodial force for the next two years. Upon completion, control of the building would pass to the governor. In this somewhat emasculated form, the bill was approved by the House on March 21, 1905, and the Senate accepted it two days later.[15]

Four days later Governor Johnson vetoed the bill, pointing out that the capitol was in use and that all state buildings were controlled by the governor. Therefore, by law and custom the act violated his legal authority and his duty. Further, he said, the Horton bill invited delay in completion of the building. The issue was thus sent back to the legislature.[16]

The Republican leadership in both chambers acted promptly. The Senate repassed the measure by the requisite two-thirds vote early on the morning of March 30, 1905, and the House "took it up without warning" on the afternoon of the same day. It passed almost without debate. The vote in both chambers was along party lines.[17]

It was clear that the Republicans intended to wait out the Democratic governor and take up the issue again under more auspicious circumstances. The Seabury-Gilbert-Horton faction felt secure for the moment; a great deal of work still remained to be completed—probably enough to last for two years since so much of the art work could not be hurried. Meanwhile, it was only necessary not to do anything to suggest in any way that it was time to give up jurisdiction of the building. When an enterprising reporter inquired about the board's plans for dedicating the capitol, Seabury replied that the ceremony "had not even been suggested among the members." The reporter speculated shrewdly that the capitol commission had "no disposition to end its existence by pronouncing the building complete."[18]

But John A. Johnson had not become the third Democrat to be elected governor of Minnesota since 1857 without learning a bit about politics, and the next victory in the game of "who controls the capitol" was his. In March 1905, the veterans of the Grand Army of the Republic came up with the patriotic idea of a special commemoration day to mark the transfer of the colors of Minnesota regiments to their special glass cases in the new statehouse. Johnson recognized the opportunity and speedily issued an executive proclamation for a special "Flag Day" on June 14, 1905.[19]

The political overtones of the occasion were quickly buried in one of those spontaneously organized American expressions of patriotism. As the veterans of both the Civil and Spanish-American wars prepared for the big day, the spirit and respect they felt for the old regimental flags permeated the city and trickled out into the countryside. Even the railroads helped by reducing the cost of a round-trip ticket to St. Paul to that of a one-way fare plus fifty cents.

The parade was even bigger than the one that had attended the cornerstone ceremony in 1898. More than a thousand veterans of the Civil War "come from distant homes to march once more and for the last time under the same old flags they had carried more than forty years ago" were joined by two regiments of army infantry, a field artillery battalion, a platoon of St. Paul mounted police,

six bands (including that of the *Minneapolis Journal*), three drum corps, and 273 young girls from Franklin School suitably costumed and arranged to represent a "living flag."

The principal address of the day was delivered by Archbishop John Ireland, who forty years earlier had served in the Civil War as chaplain of the Fifth Regiment of Minnesota Volunteer Infantry. His oration was meant to evoke the sentiments of the past. Its theme was the old flags "borne by loyal sons of Minnesota through America's mighty war, in defense of the oneness, of the life, of America, borne ever stainless and blameless, borne ever with firmest resolve to die or to conquer, borne at last to resplendent victory!" The archbishop closed his paean with a simple flourish: "Mr. Governor, the old soldiers present to your keeping the delight of their hearts—the old flags. Old flags, good bye!"

It was a moment when America felt sure of itself, when Americans did not ask questions, and when past glories could be openly recalled. The governor's response was in keeping with this spirit. The flags were carried up the steps of the new capitol and into the rotunda, where they were placed reverently in the four flag cases planned for them. The "living flag" sang "America," and the ceremony came to a close.

Throughout the day the ghost of Colonel William Colvill, leader of the intrepid charge of the First Minnesota Regiment that had saved the Union Army at the battle of Gettysburg, hovered over the entire affair. Colvill, who was seventy-five years of age, had traveled to St. Paul for the ceremony. He died there on June 12, two days before it took place. Throughout the proceedings his body lay in state in the west corridor of the new capitol near the entrance to the governor's suite. Not one of the capitol commissioners or the architect was listed on the Flag Day program. The day belonged to the citizen-soldier veterans of two wars—and to the governor.[20]

Governor Johnson won the next round too. He was re-elected in November 1906 by a landslide, defeating Republican A. L. Cole by a margin of 72,318 votes. The Democrats also picked up eight seats in the Senate, giving them a total of nineteen, or almost a third of the sixty-three senators. A political writer of the day felt that in "many cases . . . a third of the votes may well control the situation." In large part, Johnson's victory at the polls was a crushing blow to those who had dreamed of a friendly governor to help them establish a permanent capitol commission.[21]

In 1907 the capitol commissioners' relationship with Gilbert came to an end, and that gentleman, recognizing their contributions to his efforts, wrote them a long letter of praise. "I wish that the people of Minnesota," he wrote, "could realize fully what I know so well of your thorough and unselfish work in connection with this whole enterprise."

After ordering the letter "spread upon the minutes," the board considered a claim from Butler Brothers for $368.50 "for extra marble work in the Governor's Reception room." The commissioners rejected the claim, although more than $41,000 remained unexpended in their account. Other minor questions would continue to demand their attention until autumn, but at last, Frank E. Hanson, secretary of the board, would write in the minute book on September 3, 1907, "On motion the board adjourned 'sine die.'" The work was done.[22]

The men who were responsible for the job went on to their rewards. Cass Gilbert became president of the American Institute of Architects in 1908 and 1909, was appointed by President William H. Taft to the National Commission of Fine Arts in 1910, and reappointed by President Woodrow Wilson in 1914. He helped found and was president of the Architectural League of New York and was a founder of the Academy of Arts and Letters; he served as president of the National Institute of Arts and Letters, was made an honorary member of the Royal Institute of British Architects, was granted the French Legion of Honor, and was a charter member of the American Academy, Rome. He would design and build many prestigious buildings, ranging from the Woolworth skyscraper in New York City and the United States Supreme Court Building in Washington, D.C., to a delightful Episcopal church in Moorhead, Minnesota. The Minnesota capitol provided the springboard that catapulted him to an international reputation.[23]

Channing Seabury retired from the public view to give badly needed attention to his private affairs. Among the appreciative letters he received was one from Senator Knute Nelson. The "work that the Commission accomplished," Nelson wrote, "will continue a living monument to the people of our state as long as the building survives. No commission or other body that has had charge of the erection of a public building made a better record than your commission did, and while the commission as an entirety was a good one, you above all the others deserve chief credit." Channing Seabury died on October 28, 1910.[24]

The attempt, begun in 1891, to reach a decision on the location of the seat of Minnesota government by investment rather than through political processes was successful. The gigantic Renaissance palace remains Minnesota's state capitol. Erected with superb materials and expert workmanship, Gilbert's lavishly decorated edifice would be faulted by critics of a later era as failing to represent anything midwestern. If one can conceive of such a regional architectural concept, the charge is true because neither the architect, the commissioners, the legislature, nor the citizens wished the building to be "midwestern." The one clear intent from the day of the capitol's inception was to construct a building that would demonstrate that Minnesota was no longer a rural state on the edge of the frontier, that it had reached the stage of civilization distinguished by urbanization. The capitol would also be criticized as impractical. If this means that the design could not easily be altered to fit the changing needs of government, this charge is also true. Gilbert's design aimed for a visual impression that would recall traditional feelings of dignity and create a sense of continuity with the ages, belying the state's youthful chronological age. The Minnesota capitol stands as a monument in stone to a past moment in the state's history; it was and is true to itself and to its time.[25]

Gilbert's third and last sketch for a grand capitol approach, 1931

Living Flag choir in the parade from the old to the new capitol, 1905

Appendix A · Contents of the Minnesota State Capitol Cornerstone

The following is from *Proceedings at the Laying of the Cornerstone of the New Capitol of Minnesota on the 27th Day of July, 1898, at the City of St. Paul*, 30 (St. Paul, 1898):

In the sealed and soldered box that lies in the cornerstone the following articles were placed, to lie for unknown hundreds of years:

Holy Bible.
Statutes of the State of Minnesota, Vols. 1 and 2.
Last published annual report of the Minnesota secretary of state.
Last published annual report of the Minnesota state auditor.
Last published annual report of the Minnesota state treasurer.
Legislative manuals of Minnesota for the years 1893, 1895 and 1897.
History of Minnesota Volunteers in the War of the Rebellion, Vols. 1 and 2.
Minnesota Historical Society Collections. Vols. 4 and 8.
Minnesota Historical Society publication, *How Minnesota Became a State.*
Congressional directory of the Fifty-fifth Congress of the United States.
History of the new capitol legislation.
The original draft of the bill drawn and introduced in the legislature by Hon. William B. Dean of St. Paul, for the erection of a new capitol.
Edward D. Neill's *History of Minnesota.*
History of the Sioux War of 1862–63, by Isaac V. D. Heard.
Minnesota Year Book for the years 1852 and 1853.
Photographs of the new capitol.
Photographs and engravings of Minnesota cities and villages.
Minneapolis through a camera.
Copies of the last issued daily newspapers of St. Paul and Minneapolis.
Badge of the Daughters of Veterans, Tent No. 1, St. Paul, Minn.
Report of the Grand Army of the Republic for Minnesota.
American flag and roster of St. Paul Camp No. 1, Sons of Veterans, U.S.A.
One $20 gold coin, one $10 gold coin, one $5 gold coin, and one each of all the silver, nickel and copper coins of the United States of this date.
Portrait of Alexander Ramsey, first governor of the Territory of Minnesota.

Portrait of Henry Hastings Sibley, first governor of the State of Minnesota.

A copy of the introductory address by Hon. Charles H. Graves.

A copy of the oration delivered today by Hon. Cushman K. Davis.

Copper plates of the seal of the Territory and the State of Minnesota.

Copper plate etchings of south front elevation and principal floor plans of the capitol.

A copper plate on which are engraved the names of the capitol commissioners, secretary, architect and assistants.

A copper plate on which is engraved an epitome of memorable events in the history of the organization of the Territory and State of Minnesota.

City Directory for the year 1898 of St. Paul, capital of Minnesota.

Northwestern Gazetteer and Business Directory.

A list, engrossed on parchment, of the contents of the cornerstone.

A copy of the program and ceremonies of laying the cornerstone.

One of the copper plates deposited in the stone bears the following inscription:

Epitome of Memorable Events in the History of the Acquisition and Organization of the Territory and State of Minnesota.

1784. March 1—Cession by the State of Virginia to the United States of that portion of Minnesota lying east of the Mississippi river.

1803. April 30—Treaty concluded with France for the cession of Louisiana to the United States, embracing that portion of Minnesota lying west of the Mississippi river.

1805. Sept. 23—Conferences with different bands of Indians.

1837. Feb. 18—Convention with Wahpaakootah and other Sioux Indians.

1838. June 15—Treaty with Chippeways, by Henry Dodge, proclaimed.

1838. June 15—Treaty with Sioux, by J. R. Poinsett, proclaimed.

1838. The first pre-emption claim to land at St. Anthony Falls made by Franklin Steele.

1849. March 3—The United States Congress passed the organic act creating the Territory of Minnesota.

1849. June 1—The governor, Alexander Ramsey, by proclamation, declared the Territory duly organized. Population, 4,940.

1853. Feb. 24—The treaty of Traverse des Sioux, made by Alexander Ramsey and Luke Lea, with the Sioux Indians, on July 23, 1851, and the treaty of Mendota, made by Alexander Ramsey and Luke Lea, with the Sioux Indians, on Aug. 5, 1851, were proclaimed by the president.

1857. Feb. 26—The act authorizing the territory to form a state government passed by Congress.

1857. Oct. 13—A state constitution was adopted.

1858. May 11—Congress passed the act admitting Minnesota into the Union, Henry Hastings Sibley being the first state governor. Population, 150,037.

1862. July 2—The first railroad in Minnesota was operated, the train running from St. Paul to St. Anthony.

1861 to 1865—Minnesota furnished more than 25,000 men for the War of the Rebellion.

1890. June 1—Population, United States census, 1,301,826.

1895. June 1—Population, state census, 1,574,619.

Appendix B · Original Murals and Paintings in the Minnesota State Capitol

ROTUNDA

Civilization of the Northwest (four panels) by Edward E. Simmons
Twelve Signs of the Zodiac with accompanying decoration by Elmer E. Garnsey

GOVERNOR'S RECEPTION ROOM

The Treaty of Traverse des Sioux by Francis D. Millet
The Second Minnesota Regiment at Missionary Ridge by Douglas Volk
The Third Minnesota Entering Little Rock by Stanley M. Arthurs
The Fourth Minnesota Regiment Entering Vicksburg by Francis D. Millet
The Fifth Minnesota at Corinth by Edwin H. Blashfield
Father Hennepin at the Falls of St. Anthony by Douglas Volk
The Battle of Nashville by Howard Pyle
The Battle of Gettysburg by Rufus F. Zogbaum

EAST STAIRCASE LUNETTE (above entrance to Supreme Courtroom)

The Contemplative Spirit of the East by Kenyon Cox

WEST STAIRCASE LUNETTE (above entrance to Senate Chamber)

Yesterday, Today, and Tomorrow by Henry Oliver Walker

STAIRCASE LUNETTES (at base of skylight vaults)

Minnesota Industries: *The Dairy Maid, Horticulture, Stonecutting, Logging, The Huntress, Sowing, Milling, Mining, Winnowing, The Pioneer, Commerce,* and *Navigation* by Elmer E. Garnsey, designer; Arthur R. Willett, painter

HOUSE OF REPRESENTATIVES CHAMBER

Records and History (from a Cass Gilbert sketch) by W. A. Mackay *(no longer visible)*

HOUSE RETIRING ROOM

Frieze above wainscoting depicting Minnesota flora by Elmer E. Garnsey

RATHSKELLER
Decorative paintings and German mottoes by Elmer E. Garnsey, designer

SENATE CHAMBER
The Discoverers and Civilizers Led to the Source of the Mississippi by Edwin H. Blashfield
Minnesota the Granary of the World by Edwin H. Blashfield

SENATE CHAMBER PENDENTIVE MURALS
Freedom, *Courage*, *Justice*, and *Equality*, by Elmer E. Garnsey, designer; Arthur R. Willett, painter

SUPREME COURTROOM
The Relation of the Individual to the State by John La Farge
The Recording of Precedents by John La Farge
The Moral and Divine Law by John La Farge
The Adjustment of Conflicting Interests by John La Farge

MISCELLANEOUS
Throughout the building, ceilings and arches are decorated with designs by Elmer E. Garnsey.

Kenyon Cox's mural *The Contemplative Spirit of the East*, above the entrance to the Supreme Court chamber, 1905

Recommended Reading and Notes

RECOMMENDED READING

Geoffrey Blodgett, *Cass Gilbert—The Early* Years (Minnesota Historical Society Press, 2001)

Thomas O'Sullivan, *North Star Statehouse* (Pogo Press, 1994)

NOTES

Prologue—*pages xi to xiv*

1. Exceptions to this generalization may be found in some of the original thirteen states, which have kept their pre–Revolutionary War colonial capitols and in the glorious monument to politically controlled architecture that is the New York State Capitol. Since Goodhue's breakthrough in the 1920s, North Dakota, Louisiana, and Oregon have avoided the tradition, and Hawaii has erected a gem.

2. *Minneapolis Tribune,* Dec. 30, 1904, p. 8.

3. See Franklin T. Ferguson, "The Cathedral of St. Paul," in *Minnesota History,* 39: 153–162 (Winter 1964).

4. Board of State Capitol Commissioners, *Biennial Report,* 1895, p. 4.

5. Board, *Biennial Report,* 1901, p. 10; *Pioneer Press,* Oct. 31, 1895; *Tribune,* Nov. 1, 1895. The *Minneapolis Journal* had doubts; see the editorial for Oct. 31, 1895.

6. Unsigned rough draft of a letter addressed to the Board of State Capitol Commissioners, Sept. 9, 1895, in the Cass Gilbert Papers, Minnesota Historical Society. The handwriting seems to be that of architect Gilbert. The final assignment of space appears to have satisfied everyone except the superintendent of public instruction, J. W. Olsen. He carried his cause to the newspapers, but apparently did not prevail even by a public appeal. See *Tribune,* Jan. 6, 1905, p. 7.

7. The classic example of the inability of American political bodies to erect public buildings is, of course, the United States Capitol in Washington, D.C. Other delightful examples of political bungling may be read in the stories of the capitols of Kansas and New York. See *The Kansas Capitol Building* (Topeka, n.d.) and Cecil R. Roseberry, *Capitol Story* (New York, 1964).

To the thirty-seven questionnaires sent out by the author (excluding the original thirteen), twenty-two states responded. The fourteen that had built capitols in the nineteenth century averaged seventeen years in construction time; eight built in the twentieth century averaged only six-and-one-half years, thanks to changes in the system of financing the projects. In the nineteenth century most states used a pay-as-you-go method. In the twentieth century, states drew on borrowing abilities to shorten building times. Minnesota used both systems, beginning the project with the former and finishing with the latter. The questionnaires also indicated that Minnesota spent more money on its capitol than fourteen of the other states replying. (Texas was excluded from this comparison, having paid for its building with land rather than cash.)

Chapter 1—The Site and the Design—*pages 2 to 17*

1. Details on the complex legislative history of this matter as well as on attempts to remove the capital from St. Paul to other locations may be found in the author's article, "A Half Century of Capital Conflict: How St. Paul Kept the Seat of Government," in *Minnesota History*, 43: 238–254 (Fall 1973).

2. Of the four replacement appointees to the board, Edgar Weaver served the longest and had the greatest impact. A successful businessman, he had settled in Mankato in 1879 as the agent for the J. I. Case Threshing Machine Company. See Warren Upham and Rose B. Dunlap, *Minnesota Biographies, 1655–1912*, 830 (*Minnesota Historical Collections*, vol. 14, 1912); *Journal*, Nov. 3, 1914, p. 12. On Ludwig, Shell, and the younger Lamberton, see Upham and Dunlap, *Minnesota Biographies*, 453, 698; Minnesota, *Legislative Manual*, 1905, p. 655; *Journal*, Oct. 30, 1922, p. 20; Franklyn Curtiss-Wedge, comp., *History of Winona County, Minnesota*, 278 (Chicago, 1913).

3. On Lamberton and McHench, see Upham and Dunlap, *Minnesota Biographies*, 419, 470; Curtiss-Wedge, *Winona County*, 276; *Memorial Record of the Counties of Faribault, Martin, Watonwan and Jackson, Minnesota*, 661 (Chicago, 1895); Jeremiah Clemens and J. Fletcher Williams, *The United States Biographical Dictionary and Portrait Gallery of Eminent and Self-made Men*, Minnesota, vol. 94 (New York and Chicago, 1879); Board, *Biennial Report*, 1897, p. 6.

4. On Du Toit, see R. I. Holcombe and William H. Bingham, eds., *Compendium of History and Biography of Carver and Hennepin Counties, Minnesota*, 277 (Chicago, 1915); *National Cyclopaedia of American Biography*, 6: 34 (New York, 1929); Joseph A. A. Burnquist, *Minnesota and Its People*, 4: 91 (Chicago, 1924); *St. Paul Dispatch*, Feb. 21, 1923, p. 5.

5. Albert N. Marquis, ed., *The Book of Minnesotans: A Biographical Dictionary of Leading Living Men of the State of Minnesota*, 122 (Chicago, 1907); Upham and Dunlap, *Minnesota Biographies*, 171.

6. Marion D. Shutter and J. S. McLain, eds., *Progressive Men of Minnesota: Biographical Sketches and Portraits of the Leaders in Business, Politics and the Professions*, 182 (Minneapolis, 1897); *Commemorative Biographical Record of the Upper Lake Region*, 279 (Chicago, 1905); Francis B. Heitman, *Historical Register and Dictionary of the United States Army*, 471 (Washington, D.C., 1903); *Duluth News-Tribune*, Oct. 8, 1928, p. 1.

7. Marquis, ed., *Book of Minnesotans,* 103; Upham and Dunlap, *Minnesota Biographies,* 142; *St. Paul Pioneer Press,* July 22, 1917, sec. 2., p. 4.

8. Henry A. Castle, *History of St. Paul and Vicinity,* 908–910 (Chicago and New York, 1912); Edward D. Neill; *History of Ramsey County and the City of St. Paul,* 608 (Minneapolis, 1881).

9. On the site, here and below, see Board, *Biennial Report,* 1895, p. 3–7; 1897, 3.

10. An illustration may be seen in Kansas where the state capitol was begun in 1866 and, after five delays to assure pay-as-you-go financing, was finished in 1903—at a total cost of $32,000,500. The local sandstone used to build the east wing was taken from a quarry on a farm belonging to a prominent Kansas congressman. In the first severe winter after the walls were erected, the sandstone deteriorated to the point where everything had to be torn down and the entire project begun anew. See *Kansas Capitol Building.*

11. A copy of the resolution is part of the AIA legislation Committee, "Minutes," in the Gilbert Papers. We have no way of knowing whether Gilbert had anything to do with the consideration and adoption of the resolution. When we consider the sums actually spent on the capitol project, it is tempting, but unwarranted by the evidence, to leap to the conclusion that he was the instigator.

12. Gilbert's note and Seabury's reply are in the Gilbert papers. See also Minnesota Legislature, House Committee on Public Accounts and Expenditures, *Report of the Investigation of the Capitol Commission,* 16–19 (St. Paul, 1903), hereafter cited as *Report of Investigation.*

13. *Report of Investigation,* 20; undated, unsigned memorandum to the Board of Commissioners; C. A. Reed to Gilbert, May 27, 1894; C. H. Johnston to Gilbert, Aug. 3, 1894, all in Gilbert Papers.

14. Board, *Biennial Report,* 1895, p. 5; Traphagen & Fitzpatrick to Gilbert, Oct. 23, 1894, Gilbert Papers.

15. "Report of the Expert Architects," in *Report of Investigation,* 31.

16. Board, *Biennial Report,* 1895, p. 5; *Report of Investigation,* 40, 43. Wheelwright's suggestion was not followed; the second competition was also an open one.

17. Board, *Biennial Report,* 1895, p. 6.

18. Minnesota, *House Journal,* 1895, p. 343. The Senate produced a surprise. The city of Minneapolis offered the state a downtown property valued at $2,000,000; Senator Stevens pointed out that this was an attempt to utilize the Exposition Building—a white elephant built in 1886 for the Industrial Exposition Association of Minneapolis—which had steadily lost money. Stevens invoked the 1851 agreement that had placed the prison in Stillwater, the university in Minneapolis, and the capitol in St. Paul; his argument prevailed, 28 to 17 votes. *Tribune,* Mar. 8, 1895.

19. *Tribune,* Mar. 8, 1895; Board, *Biennial Report,* 1897, p. 4; Minnesota, *Senate Journal,* 1895, p. 315.

20. *Report of Investigation,* 44.

21. E. M. Wheelwright to the Board of Commissioners, Gilbert Papers.

22. Board of Commissioners, "Minutes of Meetings," Oct. 25, 26, p. 50, Oct. 30, p. 51, 1895, in Minnesota State Archives, St. Paul, hereafter cited as Board, Minutes.

23. Gilbert Papers.

24. There must have been some second thoughts about the candor revealed in the letter, because printed copies of it make no mention of marble. See *Report of Investigation,* 59. Hindsight suggests that the idea of using non-Minnesota stone was nevertheless present at this early date.

25. *Dispatch,* Oct. 31, 1895; *Tribune,* Nov. 1, 1895; *Pioneer Press,* Oct. 31, 1895.

26. The author has been unable to confirm the *Journal's* contention of a relationship between Seabury and Gilbert.

27. Board, Minutes, Dec. 17, 1895, p. 53; Board, *Biennial Report,* 1897, p. 4.

Chapter 2—The Architect—*pages 18 to 27*

1. Quotations here and in the following paragraph are from Harris E. Starr, ed., *Dictionary of American Biography,* 21: 341–343, Supplement One (New York, 1944). The sketch was written by Egerton Swartwout, who knew Gilbert personally. For an account of Gilbert's life and career in Minnesota, see Geoffrey Blodgett, *Cass Gilbert: The Early Years* (St. Paul: Minnesota Historical Society Press, 2001).

2. Wheelock to Nelson, Mar. 4, 1893, copy in Gilbert Papers. The fair's architecture was planned by the nation's most successful craftsmen, and its eclectic domes, columns, and arches had a long-lasting effect on American architecture, penetrating "deep into the constitution of the American mind, effecting there lesions significant of dementia," according to architect Louis H. Sullivan. Sullivan's was definitely a minority opinion in 1893. One of the participating artists, sculptor Augustus Saint Gaudens, called the fair planning conferences "the greatest meeting of artists since the fifteenth century." See Wayne Andrews, *Architecture, Ambition and Americans,* 222, 223 (New York, 1955).

3. Moses P. Handy, ed., *The Official Directory of the World's Columbian Exposition, May 1st to Oct. 30th, 1893,* 70 (Chicago, 1893); Gilbert to the Board, Sept. 9, 1895, Gilbert Papers; Andrews, *Architecture,* 224.

4. Swartwout, in *Dictionary of American Biography,* 21: 341; Donald R. Torbert, "A Century of Art and Architecture in Minnesota," in William V. O'Connor, ed., *A History of the Arts in Minnesota,* 52 (Minneapolis, 1958).

5. Baker Brownell and Frank Lloyd Wright, *Architecture and Modern Life,* 58, 59 (New York, 1937).

6. Swartwout, in *Dictionary of American Biography,* 21: 343.

7. An unsigned rough draft of the 1895 contract appears in the Gilbert Papers. A penciled notation at the top, probably in Gilbert's handwriting, states that the agreement was originally prepared by De Laittre and that the penciled insertions are by Gilbert.

8. Board, *Biennial Report,* 1897, p. 16.

9. Pauline King, *American Mural Painting: A Study of the Important Decorations by Distinguished Artists in the United States,* 152 (Boston, 1902).

10. Charles R. Lamb to Gilbert, Mar. 4, 1896, Gilbert Papers.

11. *St. Cloud Daily Times,* Apr. 28, 1896. Baxter was successful in his purchase negotiations and eventually in supplying granite for the capitol. His bid was $737,000. The Baxter quarry was in the middle of a boomerang-shaped piece of real estate in the

southeast quarter of Section 24, St. Joseph Township, Stearns County. The west end of the boomerang abuts Highway 23, and there the spur track crosses the pavement and follows the curve to the quarry. The original quarry was closed and the same prospect was opened a short distance east; the pit from which the "capitol" granite was taken was filled with spalls from the new pit. Information from John C. Alexander, owner of the Cold Spring Granite Company, Cold Spring Minnesota, recorded in Glanville W. Smith to the author, Mar. 28, Apr. 8, 1972, copies in the Minnesota Historical Society.

12. *St. Cloud Daily Times,* May 1, 1896; De Laittre to Gilbert, Apr. 24, 1896, Gilbert Papers.

13. Board, *Biennial Report,* 1897, p. 5. On Shiely, see *Tribune,* Jan. 17, 1972, p. 8C.

14. George J. Grant to Gilbert, Dec. 10, 1896, Gilbert Papers; Board, *Biennial Report,* 1897, p. 6–8. The completed building would be 434 feet long, 229 feet wide, and 223 feet high.

15. Board, *Biennial Report,* 1897, p. 7, 8.

16. Seabury to Gilbert, Dec. 29, 1896, Gilbert Papers; Board, *Biennial Report,* 1897, p. 10–12, 17.

17. Board, *Biennial Report,* 1897, p. 6–9, 14.

18. Board, *Biennial Report,* 1897, p. 8, 9, 14.

19. Board, *Biennial Report,* 1897, p. 8, 9.

20. *House Journal,* 1897, p. 351, 520, 526, 544, 833, 858; *Senate Journal,* 1897, p. 277, 451; Minnesota, *Laws,* 1897, p. 118.

Chapter 3—The Politics of Public Architecture—*pages 28 to 41*

1. Board, *Biennial Report,* 1899, p. 12.

2. Board, *Biennial Report,* 1899, p. 12; De Laittre to Gilbert, May 4, 1897, Gilbert Papers.

3. Swift to Gilbert, June 11, 1897, Gilbert Papers.

4. Graves to Seabury, June 28, 1897, a copy sent to Gilbert, Gilbert Papers.

5. Board, *Biennial Report,* 1899, p. 12, 13; Gilbert to the Board of Commissioners, July 8, Aug. 18, 1897, "Letters Received, 1893–1907," in Minnesota State Archives, St. Paul, hereafter cited as Board, Letters Received. The quotations below are from the latter.

6. See chapter 1, note 24, above.

7. Board, *Biennial Report,* 1899, p. 13, 14.

8. William O. Crosby to Gilbert, Aug. 6, 1897, Gilbert Papers; Gilbert to the Board, Aug. 10, 18, 1897, Letters Received; Board, Minutes, Aug. 31, 1897, p. 130, 131.

9. Board, Minutes, Aug. 31, 1897, p. 129.

10. Board, Minutes, Aug. 31, 1897, p. 131.

11. The last statement cannot be true. Glanville Smith, designer and draftsman for the Cold Spring Granite Company since the 1920s, told the author in an interview on Mar. 23, 1972, that Gilbert was a "granite man" and that he was a consistent exponent of the use of the stone. Smith recalled that later in Gilbert's career he used Cold Spring granite from the quarries of John Cooke Company in the New York City courthouse and in numerous other buildings.

12. All quotations are reprinted in *St. Cloud Daily Times,* Sept. 3, 1897.

13. Seabury to Senator Ripley B. Bower, May 16, 1899, Board of Commissioners, "Letters Sent, 1893–1907," in Minnesota State Archives, hereafter cited as Board, Letters Sent.

14. *Legislative Manual,* 1893, p. 462; 1895, p. 462; 1897, p. 486; 1899, p. 500.

15. Gilbert to Swift, Sept. 2, 1897, and Swift's reply, Sept. 3, 1897, Gilbert Papers.

16. *St. Cloud Daily Times,* Sept. 15, 1897; copy of "Contract for General Construction of the New State Capitol Building at St. Paul, Minnesota," dated Sept. 15, 1897, Gilbert Papers.

17. *St. Cloud Daily Times,* Sept. 14, 1897; Seabury to Gilbert, Feb. 17, 1898, Gilbert Papers; Board, *Biennial Report,* 1899, p. 14.

18. Seabury to Gilbert, Feb. 17, 1898, Gilbert Papers.

Chapter 4—Laying the Cornerstone—*pages 42 to 47*

1. Seabury to Gilbert, Feb. 17, 1898, Gilbert Papers.

2. Seabury to Gilbert, Feb. 17, 1898, Gilbert Papers.

3. Seabury to Gilbert, Mar. 7, 1898, Gilbert Papers; Board, Minutes, Dec. 6, 1898, p. 163.

4. The description here and below is based on *Proceedings at the Laying of the Corner Stone of the New Capitol of Minnesota on the 27th day of July, 1898 at the City of St. Paul,* 7–9 (St. Paul, 1898), hereafter cited as *Proceedings.* For the contents of the cornerstone, see Appendix A.

5. *Proceedings,* 13, 14. The specially designed trowel was ordered from Bullard Brothers, St. Paul jewelers. See Bullard Brothers to Gilbert, July 8, 1898, Gilbert Papers. The trowel is in the collections of the Minnesota Historical Society.

6. Board, *Biennial Report,* 1899, p. 7.

7. *Proceedings,* 28, 33.

8. Seabury to Gilbert, Apr. 4, 1898, Gilbert Papers.

9. *Proceedings,* 14.

10. Saint Gaudens to Gilbert, May 26, Aug. 29, 1898, Gilbert Papers.

11. Butler-Ryan Company to Gilbert, Oct. 6, 1893, Gilbert Papers. Information on the rejected column is from an interview of the author with John C. and William M. Alexander, May 11, 1972. Their father, Henry N. Alexander, was the owner-operator of the Rockville Granite Company, which had contracted to provide four of the granite monoliths on the second floor of the capitol facing the rotunda as well as to turn and polish all eight columns. His lathe—fabricated by a forgotten basement genius, Harry Dyer, who worked for the St. Cloud Iron Works—was the only lathe in the state large enough to handle the giants. Glanville Smith to the author, Mar. 28, Apr. 8, 1972. William Alexander, an expert stone polisher, remembers the incident of the imperfect column, which had further adventures. After lying on the capitol grounds, it was taken to the St. Louis Exposition in 1904 and erected as a flagpole base. Henry Alexander later sold it to a private party for the sum of $85.00.

Chapter 5—The Dome—*pages 48 to 63*

1. Seabury to Gilbert, Nov. 25, 1899, Gilbert Papers.

2. French to Gilbert, June 12, 1899, Gilbert Papers.

3. French to Gilbert, Apr. 5, 1899, Gilbert Papers.

4. French to Gilbert, Dec. 18, 1899, Gilbert Papers.

5. French to Gilbert, Oct. 12, 1897, Nov. 26, Dec. 3, 1898, Apr. 21, June 12, Dec. 18, 1899, Apr. 13, 1900, Gilbert Papers.

6. Martin R. Haley, *Building for the Future: The Story of the Walter Butler Companies,* 3, 5 (St. Paul, 1956); Walter Butler III to the author, Apr. 12, 1972. The Butlers sold the Georgia quarry when the capitol project was finished "for as much as they paid for it."

7. Purdy & Hutcheson to Gilbert, Aug. 16, 1898; office memorandum typed by "E.S.H." to Gilbert, July 10, 1901, both in Gilbert Papers.

8. These problems and those discussed in the paragraphs below are outlined in a typed "Record of meeting Mar. 7th and 8th in office of Cass Gilbert," Apr. 1, 1901, Gilbert Papers.

9. Board, *Biennial Report,* 1901, p. 4, 17.

10. Board, Minutes, Mar. 6, 7, 1900, p. 190.

11. For information on Guastavino, see E. L. Heins to Gilbert, Jan. 21, 1896, Gilbert Papers.

12. Board, *Biennial Report,* 1901, p. 18.

13. Board, *Biennial Report,* 1901, p. 12.

14. Board, *Biennial Report,* 1901, p. 14, 15.

15. *House Journal,* 1901, p. 418, 905, 926; *Senate Journal,* 1901, p. 181, 377, 914, 998; *Pioneer Press,* Apr. 9, 1901, p. 3.

16. Aus to Gilbert, June 3, 1901, Gilbert Papers.

17. Butler to Gilbert, Aug. 24, and below, Gilbert's reply, Sept. 2, 1901, both in Gilbert Papers.

18. Seabury to Gilbert, Oct. 16, 1901, Gilbert Papers.

19. Butler to Gilbert, Aug. 26, 1902, Gilbert Papers. On the firm's name change, see Haley, *Building for the Future,* 5.

20. Baxter to Gilbert, Apr. 11, 1901; Butler to Gilbert, Aug. 10, 1901, Gilbert Papers.

21. Gilbert to Butler-Ryan Company, Aug. 17, 1901, Gilbert Papers.

22. Butler to Gilbert, Aug. 26, 1901, Gilbert Papers; Board, *Biennial Report,* 1907, p. 3.

23. Butler to Gilbert, Aug. 23, 1901, Gilbert Papers.

24. Gilbert to Seabury, Apr. 21, 1902, Board, Letters Received. See also Board, *Biennial Report,* 1903, p. 5.

25. Information here and in the paragraph below is from Board, *Biennial Report,* 1903, p. 5–7.

26. Quotations here and below are from Gilbert to Seabury, Sept. 26, 1902, Gilbert Papers.

27. Board, *Biennial Report,* 1903, p. 10.

28. Gilbert to Paul Seabury, Jan. 12, 1904, Gilbert Papers.

Chapter 6—The Legislature's Challenge—*pages 64 to 73*

1. Van Sant, *Message to the Legislature,* 1903, p. 23 (St. Paul, 1903), reprinted in *Tribune,* Jan. 8, 1903, p. 5, 11.

2. *Legislative Manual,* 1903, p. 137, 682; *Senate Journal,* 1903, p. 51.

3. *Journal,* Jan. 14, 1903, p. 14. Funds for the capitol approach area were not appropriated until Mar. 1, 1945, and actual clearance did not begin until the 1950s. See *Senate Journal,* 1945, p. 440; *Pioneer Press,* Dec. 24, 1950, p. 12.

4. *Tribune,* Jan. 16, 1903, p. 1.

5. Quotations here and in the following two paragraphs are from *Journal,* Jan. 15, p. 11, Jan. 21, p. 14, Jan. 22, p. 4, Jan. 23, p. 18, 1903. On legislative action, see *Laws,* 1903, p. 165; *Senate Journal,* 1903, p. 83, 121.

6. Seabury to Tighe, Jan. 24, 1903, Board, Letters Sent; *House Journal,* 1903, p. 108.

7. *Tribune,* Jan. 27, 1903, p. 4; *Legislative Manual,* 1903, p. 140; *House Journal,* 1903, p. 115.

8. Seabury to Gilbert, Jan. 27, 1903, Board, Letters Sent.

9. Seabury to Gilbert, Jan. 30, 1903, Board, Letters Sent.

10. *Tribune,* Feb. 3, p. 7, Feb. 5, p. 7, 1903; Seabury to Gilbert, Feb. 3, 1903, Board, Letters Sent.

11. Seabury to Gilbert, Feb. 3, 1903, Board, Letters Sent.

12. *Report of Investigation,* 5. The report did not express the unanimous opinion of the committee; Representative John F. Rosenwald of Lac qui Parle County was the lone dissenter. *St. Paul Globe,* Mar. 14, 1903, p. 1.

13. *House Journal,* 1903, p. 953–956.

14. *House Journal,* 1903, p. 954; *Dispatch,* Apr. 1, 1903, p. 9.

15. *Tribune,* Apr. 1, 1903, p. 7; *House Journal,* 1903, p. 956; *Senate Journal,* 1903, p. 748, 830.

16. Gilbert to Board of Commissioners, May 5, 1903, Board, Letters Received.

Chapter 7—The Interior—*pages 74 to 85*

1. Adeline Adams, *Daniel Chester French, Sculptor,* 33–35 (Boston and New York, 1932); French to Gilbert, May 26, 1896, Feb. 4, 11, 1907, and "Articles of Agreement," May 19, 1903, all in Gilbert Papers; Julie G. Gauthier, *The Minnesota Capitol: Official Guide and History,* 12 (second ed., St. Paul, 1908). Unless otherwise noted, descriptions found in this chapter are based on the Gauthier booklet and on personal observation. A more recent look at the capitol's interior and artwork can be found in Thomas O'Sullivan, *North Star Statehouse* (Pogo Press, 1994).

2. Gilbert to Seabury, Apr. 26, 1901, Board, Letters Received.

3. Gilbert to Seabury, Apr. 26, 1901, Board, Letters Received.

4. Weaver to Seabury, June 8, 1901, Board, Letters Received; Gauthier, *Minnesota Capitol,* 14. The Kasota stone was taken from quarry No. 2 of C. W. Babcock and Company located just north of Main Street between the tracks of the Omaha and the Northwestern railroads in the village of Kasota. The company has been in operation since 1852. Stephen G. Babcock to the author, Apr. 26, 1972.

5. Gauthier, *Minnesota Capitol*, 14.

6. Blashfield, *Mural Painting in America*, iii (New York, 1913).

7. King, *American Mural Painting*, 152.

8. Seabury to Gilbert, Jan. 7, 1904, Board, Letters Sent. Blashfield made an anonymous but flattering remark about the Minnesota commission in his book, saying that "they began with doubt and suspicion, but, led by tact and wisdom on the part of their architect, and supported by their own intelligence and sincerity, they ended in enthusiastic realization of success deserved and achieved." Blashfield, *Mural Painting*, 51.

9. Gauthier, *Minnesota Capitol*, 13.

10. The chandelier has been lowered for cleaning and repair by means of a permanent winching machine on the roof of the inner dome. The electrolier hangs 28 feet into the space of the dome and weighs 2,500 pounds. It is 6 feet high, more than 6 feet in diameter, and is lit with 92 (75-watt) bulbs. Its prismatic effect comes from more than 38,000 cut-glass beads strung on wires.

11. See Gauthier, *Minnesota Capitol*, 15, 21.

12. Cox, "An Artist's Impression of the Minnesota Capitol," in *Western Architect*, 29 (Oct. 1905), reprinted from the *Architectural Record*, Aug. 1905.

Chapter 8—The Painters—*pages 86 to 95*

1. Gauthier, *Minnesota Capitol*, 13.

2. For a complete list of artists and paintings, see Appendix B.

3. Gauthier, *Minnesota Capitol*, 14, 22, 37, 47, 49.

4. Edith Seabury Nye, "The Men Who Built the Capitol," 11, typescript of a talk delivered before the New Century Club of St. Paul, Jan. 22, 1936, in the Minnesota Historical Society library.

5. Nye, "Men Who Built the Capitol," 17.

6. Gauthier, *Minnesota Capitol*, 43; Nye, "Men Who Built the Capitol," 12.

7. Board of Commissioners, Contracts, Sept. 28, 1903, in State Archives; Seabury to La Farge, July 8, 1904, Board, Letters Sent.

8. La Farge to Seabury, July 16, 1904, Board, Letters Received.

9. Seabury to La Farge, July 31, 1904, Board, Letters Sent.

10. Seabury to La Farge, Aug. 12, 1904, Board, Letters Sent.

11. Seabury to Gilbert, Aug. 30, 1904, Board, Letters Sent; Board, Minutes, Dec. 6, 1904, p. 371; Mitchem to Seabury, Oct. 12, 1904, Gilbert Papers.

12. Cortissoz, *John La Farge: A Memoir and a Study*, 181 (Boston and New York, 1911).

13. Gauthier, *Minnesota Capitol*, 26.

14. Seabury to Volk, Aug. 12, 1904, Volk to Gilbert, Aug. 15, 1904, Gilbert Papers. On Mayer, see Bertha L. Heilbron, "Frank B. Mayer and the Treaties of 1851," in *Minnesota History* 22: 137–140 (June 1941).

15. Pyle to Gilbert (telegram), Apr. 9, 1905, Gilbert Papers; Gauthier, *Minnesota Capitol*, 34.

16. Board, *Biennial Report*, 1905, p. 8; *Tribune*, Jan. 8, 1905, p. 8.

Chapter 9—The Capitol Completed—*pages 96 to 107*

1. Board, *Biennial Report*, 1903, p. 16, 1905, p. 3–5, 9. For the opening of the capitol to the public, see Prologue, above.

2. Board, *Biennial Report*, 1907, p. 6, 7.

3. Board, *Biennial Report*, 1907, p. 8.

4. Board, Letters Received.

5. Board, *Biennial Report*, 1905, p. 12. Ignoring the board's earlier experience, the building was cleaned by sandblasting with unfortunate results between 1937 and 1940. Information from Fred Denfeld, director of public property from 1939 to 1968.

6. Seabury to Gilbert, Aug. 26, 1904, Board, Letters Sent; L. B. Vollmer to Gilbert, Dec. 13, 1904, Gilbert Papers.

7. *Tribune*, Jan. 6, 1905, p. 7.

8. Seabury to Gilbert, Aug. 24, 30, 1904, Board, Letters Sent.

9. Memorandum by Gilbert, Apr. 9, 1905, Gilbert Papers; *Tribune*, Dec. 28, 1904, p. 5.

10. "Memorandum Relating to Development of Approaches to the Minnesota Capitol, St. Paul," Dec. 6, 1904, p. 3, 5, Gilbert Papers.

11. Lewis Mumford, *The City in History: Its Origins, Its Transformations, and Its Prospects*, 392 (New York, 1961).

12. Board, *Biennial Report*, 1905, p. 12.

13. *Tribune*, Jan. 17, 1905, p. 7; *Senate Journal*, 1905, p. 26, 73, 76, 504, 525.

14. Seabury to O. H. Ingram, Feb. 9, 1905, Board, Letters Sent.

15. *House Journal*, 1905, p. 830; *Senate Journal*, 1905, p. 524; *Tribune*, Mar. 22, 1905, p. 7.

16. *Senate Journal*, 1905, p. 585; *Tribune*, Mar. 28, 1905, p. 7.

17. *Tribune*, Mar. 31, 1905, p. 5; *Senate Journal*, 1905, p. 615; *House Journal*, 1905, p. 1043.

18. *Tribune*, Mar. 30, 1905, p. 7.

19. Here and four paragraphs below, Committee on the Flag Day Ceremonies, *Transferring the War Flags from the Old to the New Capitol* (St. Paul, 1905).

20. A bronze statue of Colvill would be the first placed in the niches of the four piers that reach up to support the capitol dome. Designed by Mrs. George J. Backus of Minneapolis, it was commissioned by the Colvill Monument Association and was unveiled on Mar. 31, 1909. See William W. Folwell, *A History of Minnesota*, 2: 314 (St. Paul, 1961). On the architect's frustrating role in the placement of this statue, see Gilbert to John A. Johnson, Jan. 20, 1908; to C. B. Heffelfinger, Apr. 9, 1908; to George H. Carsley, Jan. 14, Nov. 7, 1908, all in Gilbert Papers. Three statues of other military heroes were added in 1910, 1911, and 1914: Colonel Alexander Wilkin of the Ninth Minnesota, Colonel John B. Sanborn of the Fourth Minnesota, and Major General James Shields, who had been elected to the U.S. Senate from three different states. See Gauthier, *Minnesota Capitol*, 19 (revised edition, St. Paul, 1939).

21. *Legislative Manual*, 1907, p. 486; *Tribune*, Nov. 9, 1906, p. 7. In 1967 a capitol area architectural and planning commission was finally established, and four years later an act relating to the capitol authorized "the Minnesota state historical society to preserve the historical features" of the building, including all works of art. See Minnesota, *Laws*, 1967, p. 2058; 1971, p. 1299.

22. Board, Minutes, Feb. 5, 1907, p. 441, 442, Sept. 3, 1907, p. 448.

23. Torbert, in O'Connor, ed., *A History of the Arts in Minnesota*, 52.

24. Nelson to Seabury, Dec. 26, 1907, Channing Seabury and Family Papers, Minnesota Historical Society.

25. The criticisms are expressed by Torbert, in O'Connor, ed., *Arts in Minnesota*, 51.

Capitol Boulevard, 1905

Index

PHOTO CREDITS:

The color rotunda photo is by Mark M. Nelson, former Senate Media Services photographer; the color Supreme Court and Rathskeller views are by Eric Mortenson, MHS. All the other color photos are by David J. Oakes, Senate Media Services. The black-and-white images (excluding French in his studio, which is courtesy the Smithsonian Institution, and the capitol approach drawing from the Library of Congress) are from the Minnesota Historical Society collections, St. Paul (including undated newspaper clippings and drawings from the Board of State Capitol Commissioners Papers, State Archives, and the capitol competition drawings from the *St. Paul Dispatch*, Oct. 8, 1895).